When living seems complex, answers hard to find, this luminously glowing book opens up new directions of thought and vision. Experiencing a fresh 'take' on reality is to transform your surroundings and the ways you relate to them.

Boundaries of life and death retreat before an affirmation of the wonder of existence in a bountiful world, as writer-medium Dilys Gater and her researcher husband Paul take the reader on a unique journey through a summer of discussion and discovery in company – and conversation - with one of the greatest of English composers.

Dilys Gater is the author of over 90 books, whose work is respected worldwide. Paul Gater, a horticulturist and writer, achieved success in the UK and USA in 2003 with his investigation into *Living with Ghosts*.

Sir Arnold Bax (1883 – 1953), English Romantic composer of a wide range of orchestral, choral and chamber music, was noted for the emotional colour, depth and passion of his work. A virtuoso pianist, he was also a gifted writer, raconteur and wit.

'Mind-blowing – Bax is an utterly fascinating character'
George Telfer
Gielgud – A Knight in the Theatre

*'This is a journey, a travelling through the summer,
revisiting some of the places that I loved
and sharing some of my image pictures'*
Bax

SUMMER WITH BAX

A fresh take on reality

DILYS GATER
with PAUL GATER

ANECDOTES
2006

Paperback
ISBN 1-898670-09-9
9 781898 670094

A CIP catalogue record for this book
is available from the British Library

Published by Anecdotes,
38 Grosvenor Street, Leek, Staffs, ST13 5NA

Printed and bound by
The Basingtstoke Press,
Digital House, The Loddon Centre, Wade Road,
Basingstoke, Hants, RG2 8QW

PHOTOGRAPHS BY MARK BORG

Portrait of Ellen Kent
by Ellen Kent Opera & Ballet International
Portrait of Arnold Bax by Paul Corder
(By kind permission of Graham Parlett)
HE WISHES FOR THE CLOTHS OF HEAVEN
by W B Yeats
(Reproduced from Selected Poetry *by W B Yeats,
Pan Books, by permission of A P Watt Ltd on behalf of
Michael B Yeats)*

CONTENTS

Ellen Kent: 'All my productions create a lot of reaction...
I want to explore, go where others haven't been. I want to
give people something they have never had before...
I believe beauty heals, colour heals – the sounds,
the whole sensuality of the experience. I aim to
put on my stage something that makes people happy'

FOREWORD

It is with a great sense of pleasure that I have read *Summer with Bax* by Dilys and Paul Gater. I found the book as inspirational as meeting with Dilys and Paul during my visit to the Midlands with *Madama Butterfly* this year.

I have always been aware of the rich spirituality of flowers and colours against a background of inherent music that is all around us.

Dilys seemed surrounded by an aura of a beautiful, deep, tranquil sea green, which is how I will always think of her and her soul radiating this glimpse into another reality of richness and peace.

ELLEN KENT
Opera and Ballet International
London, October 2005

HE WISHES FOR THE CLOTHS OF HEAVEN

Had I the heavens' embroidered cloths,
Enwrought with golden and silver light,
The blue and the dim and the dark cloths
Of night and light and the half-light,
I would spread the cloths under your feet:
But I, being poor, have only my dreams;
I have spread my dreams under your feet;
Tread softly because you tread on my dreams.

William Butler Yeats
(By kind permission A P Watt
on behalf of Michael B Yeats)

From: The Garden of Proserpine

From too much love of living,
* From hope and fear set free,*
We thank with brief thanksgiving
* Whatever gods may be*
That no man lives for ever,
That dead men rise up never;
That even the weariest river
* Winds somewhere safe to sea.*

Algernon Charles Swinburne

Dedicated to the production team
Jane for wisdom and enthusiasm
Mark for illumination and illustration
Paul for back-up, research and solid support

Bax for being there
and for being himself

*

With thanks for their help to
David Cliffe, David Hunt, Brian Johnson, Alan F Lyford
and to Frank Borg for graphics

INTRODUCTION
How the 'conversations' were written

Dilys Gater, a practising medium, made contact with Bax in trance sessions that were fully documented and recorded.

'People who claim to have no belief in the world of spirits, of whatever sort, are entitled to their opinion, but might as well stop reading here and now,' she says. 'The broader-minded will hopefully appreciate that mediumship is a gift, in the same way perhaps that an aptitude for music or painting is a gift – it puts one in touch with other, deeper and more meaningful truths that help to illuminate the banality of our everyday existence.

'I have never felt personally that how the procedure works, or where the illumination comes from really matters: it is there, and without it, our lives would be immeasurably the poorer. So far as this book is concerned, Paul and I are making no attempt to present 'proof' of anything – though obviously, wherever relevant corroborative detail about Bax has come to light, we have included it. We feel what is important is that we have had the privilege of spending a summer in the company of a man of great artistic stature who, as we came to know him, revealed an unexpected capacity for self-examination and humility; who was not afraid to admit to human flaws; who was wonderful company, a travelling companion revealing himself to be wise as well as witty. We have been inspired by our discussions on the nature of life and of living creatively – sharing aspirations, dreams and challenges with an original mind that was the hallmark of one of the foremost composers of his day.'

Dilys, a 'mental medium', makes contact with the spirit world by focusing her concentration; no dimmed lights, sitting in circles or special conditions are required. For the sessions described in this book, she and her co-author/researcher husband Paul simply sat down quietly with a tape recorder.

'I had prepared myself on a deeper level for some days before each session, carrying out internal disciplines that naturally, were not visible to anyone else. When we came to do the sessions, I sat comfortably relaxed, closed my eyes and passed into a light trance. I connected within minutes with Bax, and just spoke aloud the communications as he gave them to me. Because I am not a 'direct voice' medium, my voice does not change, so the results sound as though I am holding a conversation on the phone, relaying messages and comments from the other end.

'The three of us each did our bit, and the results must be taken on their own merit – though Paul and I want to emphasise that any flaws or weaknesses have occurred at our end, and not where the most interesting concepts originated, with Bax. Far from being a grim kind of 'message from the dead', we found his communications a unique and vital wake-up call to life, a testament to the great joy and wonder of being alive in our beautiful world.'

The Sick Rose

O Rose, thou art sick!
The invisible worm
That flies in the night,
In the howling storm,

Has found out thy bed
Of crimson joy:
And his dark secret love
Does thy life destroy.

William Blake

1
STOP OFF
AND SMELL THE FLOWERS

'Don't keep a shut mind – be prepared to think about,
think around'
Bax

This poem was published as the work of a very young, enthusiastic writer. When I wrote it, I thought it made a deep and profound statement about time and history, life and love – about reality, really.

A Bracelet dug up by Archaeologists c. 100AD

Handle me gently, for I am old and frail,
Studded not with jewels but with memories.
My life came from white agony of fire –
A goldsmith in Deva fashioned me.
I have been held in strong masculine hands,
Gently and tenderly held by Marcus Aurelius
And lingeringly kissed by his young lips…
I carried the message of his passion,
For my circle of gold was pure and true
As his love for the beautiful Maura.

I graced her slim arms, fair as befitted a prince's daughter,
Jealously guarding on their wedding day, the beat of her pulse,
Fierce with the turbulence of love in her proud heart.

Their sons reached imperious baby hands towards me

And their daughter loved me with gentler affection –
But to them I remain always true, though they have gone,
He to roam with the Shades in Elysium,
And her dark, wild beauty to serve stranger Celtic gods.
I remain, and their love clings about me still,
Undying as my circle of fine gold.

Actually, it did have a certain amount of depth. It gives the story of the lovers as reconstructed by the archaeologist; the factual story as it really was; the story as the bracelet remembers it; the story from the point of view of each of the participants.

Confusing? To some people it might seem so. Yet any writer – especially, as I became later, a novelist – is constantly encapsulating different glimpses, different 'takes' on life, rather as a photographer shoots pictures from different angles. My own forty or so novels have 'snapped' many differently angled scenarios for my characters, few of which bore much resemblance to events as they have happened in my own life. Art, whether literature, music, painting, theatre, is something very different. It has to be otherwise it is not art - more in the nature, maybe, of news reporting.

Hamlet's famous and often-quoted advice to his actors – 'Hold, as 'twere, the mirror up to nature' – cannot be taken literally. Art does not mirror nature, reflecting it faithfully. It gives us instead a 'take' on reality - the way things are - that perhaps we have never previously glimpsed, and though we may know in our hearts that this is not necessarily the complete answer, it can help us to cope with reality as we experience it ourselves.

A writer, artist or creative person is taught this as part of his training, it is a technique needed for his work - but every human being does it unconsciously all the time. We change our viewpoint, alter our perspective, adopt a new slant, a fresh 'take' on situations or relationships. It is necessary for survival: if we can't – or won't - do it, we do not just lose out but discover that without the ability to adapt, to be flexible, life becomes seriously difficult, if not impossible.

In the ten years I have practised as a psychic and medium, counselling members of the public, I have gained a wide insight into needs that my 'psychic' books, (though these are based on my own experience and continuing personal development) actively aim to address. What seems to be most lacking in a material age where core values have been seriously undermined in culture and community, is any genuine awareness of an acceptable spiritual dimension. People look for guidance to comfort and reassure them in a difficult and dangerous world - but what is not commonly realised is that all the authoritative teachings we have, whether religious or secular, can necessarily give only their own limited 'take' on reality.

This is very much a modern problem. In 1965, when he had just written his masterpiece *The Jewel in the Crown*, the author Paul Scott commented on how modern literature would be affected by the sweeping changes then taking place in society. He defined the culture of the time – the 'Swinging Sixties' - as 'the culture of an intensely narrow age, masquerading as latitudinarian. Free and broad of speech, mean of heart. Radical in protestation, reactionary in performance...Tolerant on the surface, violently disposed underneath. A culture and an age of disenchantment with established processes, or disenchantment with the notion that any process should ever be established again.'

Half a century further on, we live in a democracy, censorship and restrictions all but abolished. We are free and equal, we can think for ourselves, do what we like, no longer confined by the rigid social or moral codes of the past. But is this really such a good thing? - is it, even, what it seems? The fact is we are not free at all. We are ruled now by the influential few, iconic figures and their opinions forced on us

7

by the media, a comprehensive global network that drums home unmercifully its own interpretation of – its own 'take' on - every aspect of our lives.

Most people are likely to view everything – whether the serious events of the day or TV programmes presented to us in the name of 'entertainment' – without realising they are constantly being indoctrinated. Those in the teaching profession inform me the young are losing their imaginations, since these are no longer exercised; personal individuality is not encouraged, conformity and 'peer pressure' rule as the norm. Many older people are now hardly able to formulate an original thought, taking what they are given as the set-in-concrete truth and as a result finding themselves increasingly unhappy, though often they do not know why.

I have been exploring this kind of problem with the clients who consult me and for the benefit of readers of my books, for some years now, reaching the conclusion that the answers so earnestly sought often cannot be found in political or sociological teachings, even in formal religion. Many people are looking for an entirely new way forward - even a way out. It is no longer just a question of 'opting out of the rat race', or 'getting away from it all', retiring to some more acceptable place, or even a far-away Shangri-La in another country. The world has shrunk. There is no longer anywhere to go, nowhere to hide.

I had not realised just how many people feel they do not belong – or more disturbingly, that they do not want to belong. I deal with members of an increasingly bewildered, stressed, often frightened public who need, and are actively seeking solace and guidance they are not able to find.

Recently completing my latest 'psychic' book – *Understanding Star Children* – I felt I had taken the subject as far as I could, and would have been repeating myself if I had tried to write more. Having explored in some depth that sense of 'otherness', that lack of identification with a progressively

8

more distressing world that makes many individuals feel they do not have, or even want, any part in it, the answer seemed to be that there are no answers.

But you cannot just give up on living, stop the world and get off.

Out of the blue, a completely fresh slant on reality presented itself. I met up with another artist – a man who had been a musician, a composer. As a medium, I did not seek the gift of communication with other dimensions but have learned to accept and live with it: when communication was made with Sir Arnold Bax, a celebrated musical giant of the early 20th century, the fact that he had died fifty years previously proved irrelevant. The conversations following our initial contact were vibrantly alive; they revealed new horizons and provided insight into depths of experience in ways not normally possible. Reality took a huge, sideways, seismic shift.

I had been looking for answers in the portentous kind of way that recalled my mother's maxim: 'Life is real, life is earnest'. All that was left behind. Paul and I found ourselves experiencing instead an invitation to just stop off and smell the flowers – for appreciation and celebration too, are vital components of living. One can get too involved, become too clever. What a relief to start living joyously for a change, forget about trying to solve the problems of existence - simply to inhabit the moment, sharing companionship and laughter, collaborating as a group of friends.

We set off on a mental journey that took us through the beautiful countryside of the British Isles – into Ireland - exchanging ideas, talking until the small hours as we might have done in the past when as students, novice writers, we had followed the same pathway all young people tread as they challenge their destinies. We found ourselves again testing and questing, stretching our minds, 'putting the world to rights', trying out new and amazing theories in absorbing discussions of the kind that had been lost along with that fiery youth when anything is possible. Sometimes it was just Paul and I, sometimes it was with our friends Jane and Mark – but always, always it was with an awareness of Bax's presence encouraging us as we talked on, entering fresh and different realities, drinking coffee and wine, deep into the night.

We found ourselves exploring the dimensions of life and death in unexpectedly inspiring and illuminating ways. We were given insight into the many facets of the creative process, whether the creation was of an abstract work of art or music or just the day to day shaping of the individual's own existence here in the 'real' world.

As with any new acquaintance, we came to know more about Bax with each session of 'conversation'. At first, our discussions seemed to be evoking the period between the Wars, the era of which Bax was a part, the times and places he knew and described to us in rich and intense images.

'In the 1920s and 1930s – to us now, at least – the mental as well as the physical landscape was one of renewed sunshine and promise,' I noted. 'The Great Conflict of 1914-1918, which had taken such a heavy toll of its generation, was over. It was time to rebuild, to invest in the future, to savour and enjoy the present, lazy leisurely days of tea on the lawn, long twilights free from the shadow of tyranny. There were house parties, weekend gatherings of gifted and articulate young men and women who saw a brave new world lying before them and celebrated it in music, art and literature.'

This picture held deep and in some ways sombre significance. Today we are all part of the generation that, half a century after Bax's death, inhabits that future. Yet as we have seen, it seems to many no 'brave new world' but an uncomfortable and even a threatening place.

What went wrong? What happened to that vibrancy of promise, those golden dreams, the values and aspirations so cherished then, so tarnished now? Bax, who was regarded after Elgar as the foremost English composer of his time,

10

compellingly presented us with a picture of his lost country – the 'blue remembered hills' of yesteryear, 'the land of lost content', as his contemporary A E Housman phrased it. We were prompted to re-evaluate our perceptions, consider how lives might be refocused in a very different environment, how personal future might incorporate the treasured ideals and ideas of a previous generation which, surviving the shattering of its own familiar reality, was still able to look forward with hope and a steadfast belief in the essential fineness and worth of mankind.

Unknown to both Paul and myself at the start of our project – we knew very little about him at all - Bax had written an autobiographical account of his early years called *Farewell, My Youth*. This was first published in 1943, and apparently, it has always been a source of regret to commentators that so gifted and articulate a writer never followed it up with a sequel. As the summer progressed, as our 'conversations' became more complex and as Paul's research uncovered the factual details of Bax's life, I realised why this was no casual encounter. The composer had known exactly what he was doing when he made contact with a medium who was also a professional author. He needed not only a secretary to take his dictation but an editor and presenter to put his words forward. I was the instrument to hand, a hopefully appropriate tool through which he could work in order to express his later, more developed thoughts and ideas.

*

Initially, I knew hardly anything about Sir Arnold Bax. Having studied music at school - the piano until I was sixteen - I could place him as an English composer of the early 20th century, and I had heard of his orchestral tone-poem *Tintagel*. Even Paul's wide knowledge of music and musicians did not

11

then encompass much more, though he filled me in on the few facts he was aware of about this neglected composer's life and times.

Bax, it appeared, had written the musical scores for several British films, including *Malta G.C.* and David Lean's adaptation of Dickens' *Oliver Twist*. He had had a long-standing love affair with a young professional pianist, Harriet Cohen. He had nurtured deep and intuitive Celtic connections, visiting both Ireland and Scotland at various times in his life.

There was a coincidental kind of link between us, though, for more in my own line – having written plays as well as books, and trained for some years as an actress – I was aware that Bax had had a brother who was a playwright. As a thirteen-year-old schoolgirl, I had taken the role of the Princess Silvermoon in Clifford Bax's one-act play *The Poetasters of Isphahan* – written, like many of his other plays, in verse.

Even more coincidentally, my mother had once appeared in a Clifford Bax one-act play called *The Cloak* as a young girl. The scene: a rocky wilderness between heaven and earth, where three characters - An Angel, The Spirit of the Newly Dead and The Unborn Spirit – encounter each other.

'*Lost!*' My Mum would melodramatically declaim the words of The Unborn Spirit as she wandered through the rooms of our house. '*Lost! I have lost the way. Show me the path.*' This was a family in-joke I grew up with, never dreaming that, years later, I might be communicating with departed and unborn spirits myself as a practising medium. Or that many of the living individuals I encountered would be expressing this same sense of loss and request for guidance.

*

This is not the first time Bax has made contact with Paul and myself – or we with him, for it is sometimes difficult to

12

identify whether communication with the spiritual world is initiated by the medium or by the communicator. With hindsight, and in view of how this book came into being, we concluded Bax might have been trying to communicate his thoughts and messages over a lengthy period, seeking an appropriate mouthpiece.

Our first contact took place some years ago, when Paul was struggling with his writing career. I found myself 'linking in' to Bax in order to ask for his thoughts on artistic endeavour. With no clear idea of what he had looked like, I perceived the composer at this time as an elderly man, sitting at a desk in what seemed to be a library or study – even a music room, since there was a grand piano. Apparently the setting was some large country house. There were long windows with sunny green lawns outside. Often, a communicating spirit will present itself in what it feels to be the most appropriate form – and in view of the dynamic, youthful personality I was later to come to know, it seems likely that on first contact Bax must have felt he needed to put across a suitably dignified, 'elder statesman' kind of impression.

It also explains why he addresses Paul – who is no longer a 'young man' – in these terms. There must be no doubt about who is running this show.

The first encounter was not a success. When Paul tried to frame questions about composing, writing and artistic work in general, Bax sharply implied Paul was wasting his time. Paul, in his turn, took offence. If it had been possible between two worlds, I think they might have come to blows. Paul did the equivalent of stamping out of the room, though I managed to persuade him to return in another session and apologise. On the whole though, Bax was not impressed and the contact seemed to have come to nothing.

Obviously time and place were not then appropriate. Though I might have been able to function as a medium for

Bax, I needed to develop further so far as my own work was concerned in order to be able to present his communications in the most appropriate way, while Paul was not ready to provide the collaboration that was required.

By the time we met up again and this manuscript took shape, we had moved to live in a different and far more liberating environment. Paul had written two books exploring spiritual subjects that had radically changed his outlook on life, and I had reached a point where I needed to consider some completely original, fresh 'take' on reality itself. We were ready for change, ready to consider whatever new options might present themselves.

Bax was to reveal the way forward, and his words need no apology. Paul has been the researcher, delving into the facts of Bax's life and music in order to provide an authoritative background against which to set our 'conversations'. I personally feel no compulsion to read anything about him or even listen to recordings of his work. For me as a medium, the man who is speaking here is perfectly able to speak for himself, and this is the Bax I recognise.

2
IMAGES IN PICTURES
In conversation with Bax – 1

Awake! For Morning in the Bowl of Night
Has flung the Stone that puts the Stars to Flight
And Lo! The Hunter of the East has caught
The Sultan's Turret in a Noose of Light.

Edward FitzGerald
The Rubaiyat of Omar Khayyam

(**DG**: We had no idea what might emerge when we sat down to record this first session – were not even sure I would be able to make any useful contact at all. Paul had no questions ready, and his opening reference to the 'Celtic Twilight' was a random query, based on the assumption that Bax's music had been influenced by the fashionable turn of the century interest in romanticism.)

Dilys: Arnold Bax — A quite mischievous personality comes through - he doesn't like being known as Arnold, it's too straight-laced. Somebody who doesn't like being recognised. He isn't easy to find, he's hidden behind what he does. He isn't seen - . Quite happy to be interviewed. I have a younger person, a much more lively interesting person who doesn't like being thought of as an aged, stolid man.

Paul: What was it about –

Dilys: Wait a minute, wait a minute, he's saying he doesn't mind talking to me, but you, Paul, don't keep a shut mind – be prepared to think about – think around – rather than come with an idea already prepared.

Paul: Although he was British born, what was it about the 'Celtic Twilight' that so captured his imagination when he was young?

Bax: Looking back in retrospect, people are saying this, but when you're there, when I was young – when I am as I am – you don't think of it that way, you don't think of it as being captured by the 'Celtic Twilight'. The things speak to you and they run in your blood and you don't give them names; names destroy, or they fossilise, names take away the living entity of what you feel. So I only felt it – whether it was the 'Celtic Twilight' was irrelevant to me -

Bax: It was very difficult for me to put across what I felt because so many people were asleep and the sleeping often don't want to be wakened - because when they wake it's harder than being asleep and this was why I had to present the images in pictures. Not just me - It's very difficult to convey the life energies or the life or the living things except in pictures.

Dilys: For him, words didn't come into it so much, he says, because he wasn't interested in words, even if he wrote things with words in them – I don't know whether he wrote music or anything with words in them.

Bax: The words were not important to me. They were more important to others, including obviously, the other Bax. (**DG**: His brother, the playwright Clifford Bax) It was more like a living picture - a transformation – the image can be passed

18

from one mind to another – and it's this sense of richness, colour and richness, the drama of the picture. I never created pictures that were not dramatic. I think still pictures don't work. It has to be drama – you enter the dynamics, the composition of drama.

Dilys: I don't know whether he studied it, but he's very interested in drama. He says the dramatic composition of a scene is conflicts – the overlapping, the clashing of colours, the clashing of form and shape.

Bax: If I had painted, I would have painted in oils – thick, heavy, impasto.

Dilys: I think he liked oil paintings, I have a picture of (a room with) oil paintings in heavy gold frames. He says he used to – they used to do things like charades and drama, not on the stage, but there was a dramatic tradition.

Paul: This was when he was young, him and his brother?

Dilys: I think so, he's very young talking now, but he's talking as a creative person, and he's going back and remembering.

Bax: When you are this age, when you are the age I was, you do not ever know when you are young. You don't know if you're young or old, you don't question it. You simply are, and what you are and what you see or feel or connect with is what the moment holds, which is what music is about. I am neither old nor young, I am neither dead nor alive, I am what I am in the moment. This is a fascinating thing. I don't compare or contrast, but you want to know what I see, what I say –

Bax: Life and the world and living – these are trite words – I am not good with words. The experience, the truth, is so blinding, so deeply rich that you only stand and are transfixed by it and all else fades into irrelevance. I was never a very patient man, I have no time for slowness and dullness. I found it very difficult to live among – or work among - those who could not appreciate that there were dimensions beyond. Sometimes some of them were aware of it, but they couldn't see –

Dilys: He's talking about the films now.

Bax: There were people who were aware, but it was accidental, they couldn't see with the disciplines or the technique, they couldn't see through the mathematical side of it, the actual structured discipline. Only through the structured discipline can you see the complete freedom of the form. There were people who looked at it from the other way. They thought they were free, but they would never be free because they didn't understand that through the form comes the freedom. And only through the form comes the freedom.

Dilys: I have a picture of lined manuscript paper.

Paul: Would he like to have written an opera? (pause) Or, did the creative process of writing an opera ever interest him?

Dilys: The films interested him more because they are visual, and in an opera –

Bax: You can't have an opera without words. The words assume the importance – since the musical line of the singing is all-important, you cannot have an opera without words, no more than you can have a ballet without dancing.

Paul: Words were important, surely, particularly in the poetry of W B Yeats, which was important to him -

Dilys: He's interrupting –

Paul: - They did evoke –

Dilys: He's interrupting, he's saying, it is the stimulus.

Bax: The words belong to other people, they are other people's discipline, not mine. So much has been said about what one thought or did - they were not there. So often, we stand and we listen and we laugh at all the presumptions of those who tell us what we thought and did and why.

Paul: But surely, words were important in another respect. At one point in his earlier career, he wrote pieces under an assumed name.

Bax: That was easy. That wasn't real words. That was just learning, exercises. I passed through that, you have to do whatever disciplines (are necessary) – I am talking about when one becomes fully aware of the full picture. In the beginning you think you see the whole picture, and indeed you do. You see *a* picture. But beyond that picture is the greater canvas which you cannot see except by making small sketches first. If you look at painting, those small sketches, preparatory sketches may look complete, but in fact they are just exercises. You never realise when you have passed into the next stage, and you never realise when you are actually working on the final canvas. You simply work in the moment.

Dilys: He very much believes in working in the moment and taking the sensations of the moment.

Bax: You learn the disciplines to free you to do this. All great artists know this and will tell you the same. They only become able to express themselves fully once they have learned how to express themselves and do not then need to concern themselves with whether they are expressing themselves or not.

Dilys: I have a picture in my mind of bluebells or blue flowers. (**DG**: In a woodland setting, under trees)

Bax: This is the Celtic-y thing, the Celtic image. Flowers and places meant more to me. Words and pictures in your head, whether it's Yeats or whether a photograph, a painting, a description by others, still they contain nothing of the reality – the reality is something that is within oneself. The scene with the flowers – bluebells, whatever they are – and the trees – You are seeing this now because I am showing it to you and sharing it with you. What does this mean? It means that it doesn't exist or it exists everywhere or it exists for everyone or it exists in everything and this is far beyond what we can comprehend. Just take the picture and do not examine it, do not ask what are the flowers, do not ask what shade is the blue or what shade is the green, and do not ask why did they grow there, where or why, who owns this land? It's enough that it's there. The being of it is all that matters.

Dilys: I have a picture of the sea – the seashore – I think Ireland.

Bax: It's very hard to leave. The world is very beautiful and I was sorry to leave it.

(**DG**: Though this was only our first session, I was becoming aware of a strong indication that we would be working together through the summer, and had received the title of the work we were to do.)

Dilys: He's telling me not to be impatient - with you, Paul. He knows you're there, he's talking to the two of us - . He says he's quite willing to discuss. Can I ask whether there's a reason why we should do this - and should we call it *A Summer with Bax*. I think he's saying that summer is a good time. I think he liked summer, all his memories are of summer.

Bax: I enjoyed the summers - and the days. Nights are – (pause). The moods shift. I remember the days.

Dilys: I'm saying shall we call it *Summer with Bax* – I'm asking whether he likes to be called by his surname – I think he does. His first name of Arnold – I think he had a middle name, or more - but he says none of them were right.

Bax: Bax is good, it's strong, it's dramatic. I like the X.

Dilys: I think there might have been in the family a double-barrelled name, or two names together, but he says he likes just that one dramatic thing, straight out. I'm asking him about the 'Sir' – 'Sir Arnold Bax'.

Bax: Well, that was very Celtic – that was the Arthurian sword - for the Grail. It was a little bit late in the day, I'd done my Grail searches by then.

Dilys: I'm asking why is he here, why has he come, allowed us to do this.

Bax: I have to, because - . No, no because. Don't ask me. I'm here, isn't that enough.

23

Dilys: I don't think there is a reason for it, perhaps we'll get it later. He's actually laughing now - he says, we'll work one out between us. *Summer with Bax*, he thinks that sounds all right.

Bax: This is a journey, a travelling through the summer, revisiting some of the places that I loved and sharing some of my image pictures. There are no people here – they are there, but when I travelled, I could only travel alone. I could take no-one, and when I'm travelling this way, I'm alone again.

Dilys: I'm asking him about this woman, actually, I'm thinking about this woman that he loved. (**DG**: Referring to the young pianist with whom he had had a relationship; at this point we knew no further details of Bax's romantic history, not even whether he had been married)

Bax: In the end, there is only oneself, and that is the yearning soul or spirit, the questing. We were so happy, we didn't need to perpetuate this, it was all right. We have other ways to go. They went their way and I went my way, and in many ways, none of it really matters. It is important for this journey that I'm alone, to show you. Other people will have their journeys and they are not the same as mine, even those I loved -What is love? Love is the interplay between the raindrops, but in the end every drop is individual and every life touches, every piece touches, every star, every bit, every note - and the whole thing is connected, but each in its way is so much of one note played with one finger. (**DG**: See 'rain' image in Chapter 3)

Dilys: The piano - I've got him at the piano again, he's sitting in his room with the piano. He's playing the piano. I think he must have been a good pianist.

Bax: Yes, I enjoyed that. I used to perform. I was very good at performing. I could put on a very good solemn, serious face and they all sat and listened so seriously. But in my mind I was running over the cliffs, and I was free of the room and the space and the faces. It's almost like being hypnotised (**DG**: Mesmerised I think would have been the word he might have used). Your hypnotists - (**DG**: What came into my mind was Derren Brown, because that's one of the names people would recognise today) Your illusionists - they think they are so clever, but we did it all the time. When I played – we played – their eyes went round – they were all under my spell. And I loved it.

Dilys: He's enjoying himself now. He's saying you can ask him more.

Bax: (to Paul) Try to get out of your mind this solemn person, on music records. That is not what I was or am. I think I knew life – maybe I had more life than you – so the idea of some great guru – imagine you had instead come to visit you a young man – (**DG**: I have a picture of a young man with rough dark hair) - who had a twinkle in his eye and perhaps had come from somewhere where he shouldn't have been. If you'd come to dine with me, I would have given you grapes and – hedonistic things that perhaps you might not have expected.

Dilys: (to Paul) Do you want to ask something?

Paul: I don't have anything else to ask him just now.
Bax: Why ask then? Just enjoy the moment and take the moment. You think too much about words.

Paul: He felt that he could paint better in sound than writing books or poetry or even painting?

Bax: I could probably have done everything if I'd felt like doing it. But you cannot be in everything. Your discipline finds you, you do not find it.

Paul: That's excellent.

Bax: I enjoy the typewriter, which helps to focus the mind wonderfully when typing words but I do not feel the typewriter frees me. To some people, writing musical notes would be a struggle. It came easy to me and so I chose the notes rather than the typewriter keys.

Dilys: I think he had a typewriter in his room, he's got an old upright like an Underwood.

Paul: Yes, that's how I see it, actually.

Dilys: I'm seeing it now, he's showing it to me. And on his desk he's got I think a shell – (**DG**: A big, pink-peach conch-type shell).

Bax: You may look at these things but they will not matter so much as what is in my mind.

Dilys: Shall I stop now? May I return?

Bax: Tomorrow I will take you into the walled garden.

Dilys: I can see a garden with a fruit tree growing up the wall. Perhaps the walled garden tomorrow. Thank you. Thank you.

3
REALITY- WHO NEEDS IT?

'The reality is something that is within oneself'
Bax

We are inclined to think of reality as solid. It's just there. But is it? Like the images captured by a photographer, reality can change. It can be different whichever way we look at it, whichever view we want to take.

My mother's maxim that 'Life is real, life is earnest' is actually a quotation from Longfellow's *Psalm of Life*. Bax might have been aware of it as very much reflecting the joyless Victorian sentiment that, clinging on in parental admonition and the traditions of Non-conformist Sunday School teachings, must have stifled many eager young hearts in the earlier days of the last century. Just take a look:

> *Tell me not, in mournful numbers,*
> *Life is but an empty dream!*
> *For the soul is dead that slumbers,*
> *And things are not what they seem.*
>
> *Life is real! Life is earnest!*
> *And the grave is not its goal;*
> *Dust thou art, to dust returnest,*
> *Was not spoken of the soul*
>
> *Lives of great men all remind us*
> *We can make our lives sublime,*

And, departing, leave behind us
Footprints in the sands of time.
Let us, then, be up and doing,
With a heart for any fate;
Still achieving, still pursing,
Learn to labour and to wait.

All very admirable, no doubt, and full of praiseworthy aspiration, but where is there any mention of enjoyment, beauty, delight, laughter? Thankfully, Longfellow's version of the reality of life is not the only one on offer. Life, we are reliably informed by John Gay, 18th century creator of the swashbuckling *The Beggar's Opera*, is a jest; while according to the 19th century writer Charles Stuart Calverley, it is (for some at least) all beer and skittles. Innumerable popular melodies remind us, if we are tempted to forget it, that life is a cabaret, life is a roller-coaster, life is just a bowl of cherries.

Shakespeare describes thought as the slave of life, and 'self-help' manuals in plenty are only too eager to explain how we can create our own realities through positive thinking, visualisation and affirmation. If this is possible, it means reality is not some solid edifice in which we must live, it is flexible and optional. The past varies according to the individual way each person remembers it. The present, too, can seem very different to different people. Why then should it not be possible for us to leave the realities we find unacceptable and enter into other, more joyous ones?

In fact, there are unlimited realities. Many great philosophers and spiritual teachers have assured us that 'The world is what we think it is – we create our own world.' So how does the average person set about changing what seems to him the difficult and even frightening reality in which he appears to be trapped?

How does one escape out of the limits, out of the cage? Bax makes it seem so simple. If you cannot move in another

30

direction because there is nowhere to go, then you expand mentally into a new and different awareness. Out of the discipline comes the freedom.

The most important requirement is to realise that change means new experience, new perception and a new 'take' on what has previously seemed unchangeable. Even in the opening moments of our first 'conversation' Bax emphasised strongly, and kept repeating, how vital it is to keep a completely open mind. With no preconceived ideas, reality is potentially limitless – only our own narrow experience and expectation confines us. And who wants to remain in that prison?

We have to be prepared for adventure, for excitingly risk-taking thinking. Even the accepted concepts of time and place offer restrictions. Time and age mean little to Bax - there is no 'then' and 'now'. He mixes his tenses and during our 'conversations', I visualised him at various times as both a young and older man as well as in childhood. The settings he presents, too, seem to flow or melt into each other so that it is often difficult to be specific; many scenes appear as composites.

With an open mind, we can comprehend and accept any reality we choose. This does not mean we are ignoring or negating other realities, we are simply selecting the reality we wish to inhabit and to embody within ourselves.

*

Our first 'conversation' has been titled *Images in Pictures* – from Bax's own words – because images and word pictures as a means of communication play a major part in this book. The first words I noted down when I began to make a record of what was happening were:

31

I saw the splashing of great drops of rain, raindrops falling on a wide sheet of water, a lake or the sea, heavy rain, a torrential downpour, cleansing and clearing, powerful and stimulating. This was the image that gave me the link with Bax – and it happened on the day before the Midsummer Solstice.

This dramatic and powerful image provided links on many different levels, not all obvious at the start. Time, place and the moment of connection – the first day of summer - were instantly communicated; other images that came later were equally vivid and compelling.

Later, complexities were explored in much greater depth. In the first 'conversation' Bax used the fierce interplay of raindrops on water as a symbolic representation of the nature of love; he returned again and again to images of water – the sea, the ocean - to illustrate his perceptions of different aspects of life and reality. In later conversations, the 'golden sea' became his image for love as well as death.

Images and words are the tools of any professional writer, and much psychic work is conducted in images – the language of the spirit being symbolic and conceptual rather than literal. Bax composed using images in sound rather than in words, but as our work progressed, it became obvious that he was investing the word pictures he was giving me with great significance. He used them as punctuation, as linking passages, as themes, in the same way he might have used musical *motifs*. He has very much orchestrated these conversation pieces, and it is no coincidence that so many of the terms he employs are musical.

I made the first contact by focusing on Bax's name, but for subsequent sessions he provided images for me to use - the walled garden – the hotel – the lighthouse. These were the places where we 'arranged to meet', and though the meetings were purely mental ones, the settings Bax described seemed to Paul and myself to hold a strong physicality. Only after a great deal of research did we become aware these 'meeting places' had not been chosen at random, that every location had existed and had held a strong significance in Bax's life.

The dimension of time, however, assumed something of Bax's own flexibility. Though some further meetings were scheduled for 'tomorrow', our conversations turned out to be conducted at intervals of two weeks, sometimes longer.

Bax communicated in specific ways, 'linking in' with scenic images I envisaged as similar to coloured postcards, snapshots of a view or a building. These pictures signified a change of thought or the beginning of a sequence that was then explored and developed. Some sections came across as clear and direct, in his own voice, though interestingly, they are not necessarily in words he might have used when alive – the actual words of a man speaking in the early 20th century. They are couched in less formal, more modern terms. At other times, I received 'feelings' which enlarged or provided commentary on his direct speech.

His communications have structure and form, even a brief examination of the text revealing their amazing clarity and consistency. I often paused, hesitated or repeated myself as I tried to find the right word or phrase, but transcriptions of the tapes enabled us to appreciate the tautness of Bax's thoughts, the crispness with which he had dictated them. What is here is more or less exactly as we received it: only 'um's and 'er's, superfluous words, repetitions on my part have been edited out, and comments given in brackets added later in order to illuminate, explain or clarify.

4

A BRIEF INTRODUCTION TO BAX

Paul Gater

'Many times I was more alone than people realised'
Bax

I have always been an appreciative listener to music. Like Bax, I find it reflects the theatre of life and the many different moods and dramas within that life – from stirring excitement and exuberance to a spiritual sense of the sacred and profound. Music can provide moments of soothing calm in our stressful existence: it offers itself to us in every therapeutic aspect.

I first encountered the name of Arnold Bax as a teenager in the 1950s, when I heard a radio performance of the piece that is generally considered to show this Romantic British composer at his best. His tremendous orchestral tone-poem *Tintagel* (completed in 1919) is the composition of a free spirit – a gloriously powerful and tender evocation of a 'sunny but not windless summer day', as the composer described it, with Atlantic rollers pounding Cornish cliffs that are crowned by a ruined castle. There are associations here not only with Camelot and King Arthur, but also the legend of Tristan and Isolde.

During the next few years I hardly encountered Bax's name. Performances of music other than by 'mainstream' composers were difficult to find on disc then - though I do remember borrowing a scratchy LP record from the local public library of his *Third Symphony*. Then, in my early twenties, I attended a concert given by the Halle Orchestra: *Tintagel* was on the programme, and it riveted me to my seat. I felt as though I had been reacquainted with a long-lost friend and also as though I had passed through some sort of initiation. I began to feel that, contrary to received opinion, (especially since *Tintagel* has been his only piece to remain in the regular orchestral repertoire) Bax must be far more than just a 'single work' composer.

Though at the forefront of British music, particularly in the 1920s and 30s, he appeared after his death to have sunk into an inexplicable oblivion - though within two years, the author Sir Compton Mackenzie, founder of the *Gramophone* Magazine, was pleading for his wider recognition. To some extent, this neglect can be attributed to the upsurge of '*avant garde*', 'modern' music of the cacophonous 'fifties, 'sixties, 'seventies and 'eighties when most emerging younger composers were writing material based on the twelve-tone technique developed by Arnold Schoenberg earlier in the century. However there is currently a renaissance of interest in Bax's music. As his work becomes more available, we can see that this dynamic, fascinating man has something to say to the 21st century as well as to his own.

Christened Arnold Edward Trevor Bax - I'm not sure whether or not he liked being called Arnold, but his other two names don't appear to have been used by him - he has come over in these fascinating sessions not only as a composer, thinker and man of the world but as a human being of intense feeling and vulnerability, which makes him even more interesting. Dilys and I experienced a great sense of energy during our 'conversation' sessions; embodying the hope and passion of his age, Bax still seems to feel the need to pass these on to his listeners – or perhaps, they are simply the qualities of the man himself.

So much of his music wonderfully celebrates the sun-drenched summer of youth and beauty. Life teaches us that they are gone all too soon, but both his communications and his compositions are filled with a richness and vibrancy that inspire us to make our own new 'take' on the joy of living.

His exciting tone-poems are filled with romance. Their names - *Cathaleen-ni-Hoolihan, In the Faery Hills* and *The Garden of Fand* - speak of origins in Celtic and Irish legend, while *Spring Fire* and *Enchanted Summer, Morning Song* and *November Woods, The Tale the Pine-Trees Knew* took their inspirations from Greek legend, the English countryside and the Scottish and Norse traditions. All are the fruits of a broad, enquiring mind, evocations of mystical atmosphere, wind and storm, of faeries, elves, goblins, trolls and sweeping woodland idyll. As a horticulturist whose own working life has been spent in the 'great outdoors', I regard Bax as probably one of the best composers to create sound images of places - particularly wild places - and of nature.

Bax's father was nearly 40 when he was born, a gentleman whose means included financial interests in Mackintosh raincoats. His mother, 17 years younger, was a vivacious, sparkling beauty who passed on her love of the arts to her children. Mainly privately educated, son of a privileged family owning land in central London (once landowners in Surrey), Bax himself did not need to earn a living: he never held a job in any official capacity except an honorary one – that of Master of the King's Musick towards the end of his life. I particularly liked the way Bax described his knighthood (of 1937) to Dilys as 'the Arthurian sword coming a bit too late', after he'd done his own Grail searches.

He could have pursued a life of idleness, but at the age of 17 won a place at the Royal Academy of Music in London. Dilys's impression that the piano was very important to him turned out to be correct. Even as a child he possessed a marked talent for the piano, later becoming a stunningly accomplished virtuoso pianist. His gifts for composition emerged at the age of twelve when, recovering from a bout of sunstroke, he produced his first work.

As a man, he came to be regarded as unconventional in many ways, despite his knighthood and the various other honours awarded to him. Always a 'non-establishment' figure - though born to social standing and with a private income - he nevertheless chose for most of his adult life to live in rooms wherever he went, eventually renting rooms for his last few years at the White Horse Public House in Storrington, Sussex.

In 1910, in London, Bax met a beautiful young Ukrainian woman named in his autobiography as Loubya Nicolyevna Korolenko, though her real name was Natalia Skarginski. He fell hopelessly in love with her – 'a disastrous and humiliating adventure' he later called it. Accompanying her on her return home in the hope that she would accept his proposal of marriage, he was able to stop off in St Petersburg on their outward journey and experience Russian art and culture at first-hand - Russian music, the Imperial ballet, and the visiting Moscow Arts Theatre Company in Chekhov's *The Cherry Orchard*. Once back in the Ukraine, however, Natalia turned down Bax's proposal, accepting that of someone else. Humiliated and dispirited, he left Russia and never saw her again.

It seemed the episode was over and he could move on, culturally enriched by the St Petersburg experience. But in fact, the emotional impacts both of his romantic idealism and of Natalia's rejection never left him and seem to have coloured all his future entanglements with women. When soon afterwards he married Spanish-born Elsita Sobrino, daughter of Carlos Sobrino, an eminent pianist of the day, it was on the rebound and set the pattern for further relationship difficulties. He felt unable to settle in London, restlessness drawing him westwards.

Back in 1905, after graduating from the Royal Academy of Music, Bax had visited Ireland with his brother Clifford, immersing himself in the Irish language, history and way of life - a result of reading and being influenced by the poetry of W B Yeats, particularly *The Wanderings of Usheen*. Regarding himself as an 'honorary Irishman', he had spent much of his time alone in the remote west, visiting wild and stormy places, sometimes by rickety boat – even areas rarely frequented by the Irish themselves. Sympathetic to the Irish Cause, he had met and befriended many different people in Dublin's literary and political circles. His intimates included the founder of the *Irish Review*, the writer and poet Padraic Colum, and Padraig Pearce, Principal of St Enda's College, Rathfarnham - an Irish Patriot who was to play a part in the 1916 Easter Rising.

Under the pseudonym of Dermot O'Byrne, Bax even wrote his own poetry and fiction – in Ireland many regarded him as an author rather than a composer. In 1907, while in Donegal, he wrote a five-act play based on the Irish legend of *Deirdre of the Sorrows*, intending to use it as the libretto for an opera but later abandoning the idea.

It was to Ireland that he took his wife after their marriage, and where his two children Dermot and Maeve were born – significantly, they were both given traditional Irish names. But the creative artist in Bax felt constrained, stifled, destroyed by domesticity and he could not survive unless free to pursue his soul's quest. Eventually he left his wife and children, though he continued to provide for them. As he put it in these conversations: 'They went their way and I went my way... Other people will have their journeys and they are not the same as mine, even those I loved.'

There were to be other 'muses', inspirational figures and companions in his life as well as a large circle of friends both personal and professional. Ultimately though, Bax appears to have always felt as though he travelled alone.

5
THE WALLED GARDEN
In conversation with Bax – 2

Iram indeed is gone with all its Rose
And Jamshyd's Sev'n-ring'd Cup where no-one knows;
But still the Vine her ancient Ruby yields,
And still a Garden by the Water blows.

Edward FitzGerald
The Rubaiyat of Omar Khayyam

Dilys: I'm going back to the room where I first saw him – in a country house - to link in – I'm going back to the rain – would you like to ask something?

Paul: At the ending of the last session, he mentioned the walled garden. I'd be very interested to hear more about it and where it actually was – what it stood for.

Dilys: I caught a glimpse of it – an espaliered tree – I don't think it was the same as the country house – . I'm still waiting for him to speak to me – he's not in the same place as he was before. He's not in that room - (**DG:** With the piano, desk and shell) - and he's not doing the same things.

Bax: I was always very unexpected. I don't like to be predictable. You're anticipating perhaps what you expect and not what is.

41

Dilys: I'm trying to find what he's doing and where he is. I don't know why he's so quiet. He's saying nothing, though he has been telling me things earlier - I think he used to like playing games, or playing tricks on people. I might have got him at another age, I'm just trying to link in - I'll go back to the garden. Here's the garden.

Bax: Communicating isn't easy. This isn't as easy as perhaps you thought. It's been an effort for me. Composition was never easy. A lot of things were, but the actual communications aren't.

Dilys: We're not really ready yet, he's telling me something else, not about the garden - it could have been a work he didn't write, or that he wrote but wanted to redo later. I think perhaps he was going to write something about a garden – maybe did – He says, a walled garden is very predictable. It's not exactly your 'Celtic Twilight' but it's certainly your 'English country garden' cliché thing.

Bax: I always used to like to explore where others didn't go. I don't like my work to be predictable, I don't like it to be what people expect.

Dilys: I think in his music he may have used unexpected pauses or done unusual things – you'd have to check on this, Paul.

Bax: I was never understood properly. I was taken for what I seemed.

Dilys: I think he was good-looking. He's saying he always managed to get round people or get what he wanted because of his looks. But he says it's very difficult to present the core of things when people only take what they see. (Pause) I think the garden might have been by the sea.

Bax: The walled garden didn't exist as such. It's partly in existence but it's partly an idea, an image.

Paul: Can I ask, is this some sort of reference to the legend -

Dilys: (interrupting) The Garden of the Hesperides. I've got the Garden of the Hesperides - the western garden - the western isles -

Paul: Does this have any connection to his tone-poem *The Garden of Fand?*

Bax: You know more about it than she does. She thought she knew me well, but you're beginning to start understanding me better. The western garden – yes.

Dilys: The tree is important too. He says the tree that I'm seeing, the image of a tree against a wall, it's spread out like this (demonstrates, see Fig. 1, end of this chapter) – the way it does – yes?

Paul: Yes.

Dilys: - It's very similar to the Tree of Life (see Fig. 4). I don't know what the Garden of Fand is, but he's saying that the tree is the Tree of Life, or it is *a* tree of life, and this is very important, this shape - the growth upwards and the lines coming out. I'm not seeing the rest of the garden, only this tree and the wall. He says the important thing is the growth. The importance is that it's a walled garden, it can be explored privately, quietly and at one's leisure but he says the tree is the

43

shape of the growth process. It's the way that maybe his music grew. He's talking about the process growing and expanding, as it rises up, it goes onto fresh levels - Now there might be levels in his work. The levels are reached as the things progress.

Bax: This interested me very much, the shape of progress. I have always been interested in steps – flights of steps – shapes -

Dilys: I'm seeing a triangular shape that comes to a point (Fig. 2); then there's the shape of the growth of the tree up the wall; and the Tree of Life. I don't know if he ever studied the Kabbala or anything to do with that, but I think he knew about it. He's saying, yes.

Bax: In my music I have explored, tried to capture these shapes. Last time I told you about drama, now I'm talking about structure. Structure and progression. I have never seen progressions proceeding from one point to another. I see them proceeding organically, they proceed more like a (**DG**: - some confusion over the word) – a hieroglyph? symbol? cipher? - than a progression in time.

Dilys: I have the sea again. I don't know which sea or where, I think it might be up in the north towards Scotland - It was the Atlantic – the Atlantic Ocean – in Ireland as well. He may have written something about the waves – Tintagel Castle I know is on the coast -

Bax: That's the ocean, my ocean is the Atlantic.

Dilys: I want to ask him about this book. Is he pleased, have we got the right idea?

Bax: Very much so. A lot of what we discovered has been lost. There were subtleties in the music I wrote – that we wrote - (**DG:** - others as well as himself). We explored avenues which were neglected or were never properly appreciated. Unfortunately every age has to discover for itself and the discoveries of the previous age have to be re–interpreted, re–explored.

Dilys: I think he might have had something to do with explorers – South America maybe? I have a picture of – Aztec images? - some kind of hieroglyphic drawings or language. It could be Gaelic – I don't know. He liked alphabets and languages.

Bax: I would have died if I had been bored. I hate boredom more than anything.

Dilys: There's a joke here, he's joking, saying well, now that I *am* dead, I'm still not going to be bored. I am following courses – (**DG:** He meant, roads or paths) - languages, directions in many other ways. I want to ask him now what his messages – these messages - are going to do for people.

Bax: Let them listen to me. If they listen to me they will know what I'm talking about. Listen to me without having ideas in your head – putting them into anybody's head. Wait to see what I have to say. There is a reason for this, and I am doing it - but how can I tell whether people will hear what I say? No more than if you write the music, you can ever tell whether people will hear. They all hear something different, and one can only speak clearly into the silence, and have the opportunity to let the message come across in whatever way. I hope there will be an audience there. I hope there is a listener. One always wanted a listener.

45

Dilys: I have a picture of him playing the piano. I think he used to do this in the evening – in the twilight – that's a bit corny, but he used to like to play in the dim light.

Bax: I was playing for whoever would listen. Playing for the trees, the birds. We exchanged performances – the birds performed for me and I performed for them. Often - I was - at a low ebb -

Dilys: He's trying to put across that he felt depressed, that he went through periods of depression.

Bax: I told you I was alone. Many times I was more alone than people realised. When people are with you, they assume you are not alone but how can they tell? Often I was alone – I had to be.

Dilys: This was not when he was young. I've got him at a later age now, maybe when he was living in Scotland. He didn't have any regular family there, he was living alone, though lots of friends, comings and goings - He says there was a time of great promise and yet of great trial - I feel it might have been when the war was on and nobody knew what was happening. He says, I wanted to be alone. I took myself into the solitude – the spaces - I've got him looking out to sea from the cliffs, or walking along by the cliffs – just looking out, waiting for something to happen - I've got a sort of sunset scene, just looking into the west.

Bax: At such times we can only send out thoughts. Call it praying if you like. I didn't call it praying. I felt that it was focusing energy and perhaps connecting with the natural world to some extent. I never took on board what people said about the natural world being the "natural world". There's no such thing as the "natural world". I saw it as a web, a great web of life -

Dilys: There might be some music he's done that would express this, and also, I think, something about nets.

Bax: - I saw it as nets, patterns again, or mosaics – I had so many ideas. I had so many images but they are all connected. If you think of a mosaic, or if you think of a net, every piece of it is so small and yet when you stand back, it becomes more and more. Each piece gets smaller and smaller but the overall picture becomes bigger and bigger. It's a concept that you could apply to living. You could see that every one – every note if you like – every one in their way is a tiny piece of the mosaic or one – just one - stitch on the net. But stand back and the webs and the nets become larger and larger.

Dilys: I think there's something here to do with whoever it was wrote about the webs - ' I have put my dreams under her feet' – the webs of – it might have been Yeats. (**DG:** Later, the poem was identified as *HE WISHES FOR THE CLOTHS OF HEAVEN* by W B Yeats)

Bax: We all felt it this way, the connections of the waves, the connections of everything. They are so interconnected. And the movement. Everything moves but it is all ebbs and flows within the basic framework. Music is the same, music is like that. Every note marks a movement and yet the movement is an ebbing and a flowing. If you – they - could see that I am just as much there as you are now, listening to me talk, whether I play a note or whether it's sung or whether it's you who feels it – These are all part of the shapes – the web.

Dilys: When he died I think he might have had chest – throat problems or suffered from weakness in this area.

47

Bax: I was disgustingly healthy. It never occurred to me that it would be otherwise. I took health for granted. I don't believe in indulging neuroses. That's a modern concept. Freud and his associates may have invented it – invented neuroses - but it's you now who actually create the neuroses out of the terrible cul-de-sacs of your life. (**DG:** He refers to life in the 21st century). The neurosis comes when the flows stop, when there is no way for the ebbs and flows to continue, when perhaps hope is cut off.

Dilys: Now I have an image of 'Land of Hope and Glory' - the Proms, which I suppose he must have known. He's saying oh yes, hope, land of hope and land of glory - People don't understand. They see hope as - And now I've got an image of a sculpture which probably exists somewhere, of 'Hope and her Children', with a laurel wreath - I think it is called 'Hope and her Children' – he knew it or perhaps he would have known the person who sculpted it. (**DG:** Seemingly of figures in white or grey marble, this has not so far been identified)

Bax: Hope is not like that, it's different. It's a light – a road into the light – a lit road, a lit way. And when the light goes out, that's when there's no hope.

Dilys: I think he was in a war, or somewhere at one time walking – trying to get through an unlit or very dangerous area - maybe had to make his way through bombing -

Bax: There are lights and lights. (**DG:** He meant, many different sorts of lights) There are lights in the dark and there are lights even when you can't see (them) – but hope is when the inner light has gone out, the spark. For me hope gone would be when I heard no sound to express. Hope gone is like a well, a water-spring, a spring of water when it has dried

48

up. This is of great concern because we tried so hard to open up the well-springs.

Dilys: I've got a picture now – not a picture, it's a feeling – an incredible sense of loss and grief which I think was what people felt, again round about the time when it would have been the First War. All the losses, the crying - and the widows - and the orphans – not the orphans – I don't know why, but I don't think he's very focused on orphans.

Bax: The loved ones who never came home.

Dilys: I don't know whether he was very good with children, I don't think there is much of a sense of him relating to children at all.

Bax: It was the ones who went and never returned. Although I don't believe in 'Celtic Twilight' and romance as such, or sentiment, I had no time for it - I'm talking about the real thing here. The people who went and did not return.

Dilys: (beginning to cry) It's a bit hard for me to say this because I can feel it all – everybody, him as well. I think they must have been very upset, they must have lost a lot of people amongst their friends. I feel that when they were having their weekend gatherings or when they met together, there was such a sense of loss and grief – this is him, not me -

Bax: Without feeling there is no music. Without feeling there is nothing – can't you see, this is what hope is, it's when the feeling is alive -

Dilys: (very distressed, crying): This is still him, Paul. It's not me. I mean, he's not actually crying, but he's really wanting to bring it over.

Bax: You must tell them this. You must show them. Crying over a neurosis is nothing, this is the real thing, and we were there. Tell them, and tell them not to lose touch with it. Tell them never to lose faith. And tell them never to lose hope. Where we are, we are back in the light, but there is no light for you now, today, down there, and only you can find the way again. Tell them never to lose faith.

Dilys: Ask him something else Paul, get him off this – I want him to get off it. He's saying there were others as well. I'm asking him who they were. He's saying you have heard of some of them, they were there. One might have been the sculptor – of Hope – and the others might have been musicians, if they were something to do with the Proms - I think that whatever problem he had with his chest, it may have been when he was in the war, or he may have suffered something – maybe he didn't die of it, but he had it at some stage – a chest thing - he could have even had an operation.

Paul: I'm not sure whether he was in the war.

Dilys: Whatever it was, they were all there.

Bax: We were all there. We saw the lights go out – all over Europe - Yes, it was true. The lights did go out. Maybe patriots do not all wave their flags.

Dilys: I think this is about the First War. He loved the country – his country - well, he loved the world.

Bax: I loved the beauty of the world. Last time I told you I was sorry to leave it. I loved the small things – living in the moment as I do. The moment is all one has. The moment is perhaps the smell of the blossom in the garden – in the walled garden. You can come into the garden now, we'll go into the garden now that what has been said is said. We can leave the melodramatics, we will walk in the garden and we will speak of ordinary things. The blossom (**DG**: pink blossom, apple blossom) – the smell of the blossom, the touch of earth, crumbling earth - This is the country that I love. You are all too sophisticated these days. Sophistication taken to extremes removes the mind from true reality and sophistication defeats itself. I was a man of the world, and so were we all. In our way, we were.

D: He's giving me a line of poetry 'O Rose thou art sick' – I know that's a poem. 'The worm that comes in the night' - . (**DG**: The poem was later identified as *THE SICK ROSE* by William Blake.)

Bax: The freshness of the world as I saw, is rotten, has a worm at the core. Think of a damask rose, there is nothing so abhorrent to nature as a worm at the core.

Dilys: I have a lovely pink, old pink rose, and he's showing me it all rotten.

Bax: The rottenness from within, the rottenness at the core is the most abhorrent to the natural order. (To Paul) Join the tea-party. We will have a civilised cup of tea here in the garden.

Dilys: It's not a garden exactly, it's a yard, a walled place but more paved. It's outside a different house, one that has got mullioned windows, quite old. Could be an ancient castle type of place. Maybe Scotland. Not the same as before, a paved yard with a wall and sun on the wall and a border and these trees (**DG**: The espaliered trees I had seen before.) But it isn't what I would call a garden, more of an area, paved stone, with moss perhaps.

51

Bax: Gardens and gardens. I was never a gardener as such. I carry my gardens in my head.

Paul: I was going to ask him if he enjoyed gardening.

Bax: I was too impatient. I could not sit back and wait for nature to fulfil its bounty. I want things to happen. It's a great sweeping drama for a gardener but it's a very slow drama. I prefer my dramas to have fireworks in them, and trapdoors and jumping jacks and clashes of cymbals to make you jump.

Dilys: I want to ask him about the music where he is.

Bax: All music is the same. Don't ask me about the Music of the Spheres, because you might as well be asking me about the Dance of the Comedians. Jugglers, whether they are juggling with balls or whether they are juggling with planets, the principles are all the same.

Dilys: Mathematics was very interesting to him. I have a sense of geometrical shapes. I think he must have gone to a public school, or privately educated, he was taught mathematics – I suppose everybody was – he liked shapes. Geography as well, because of the explorers - he might have known somebody who was an explorer. The shapes are like triangles – pyramids - . Something like an egg-timer that goes to the middle and then opens out again (Fig. 3) and changes. He says he uses that a lot in his work. (Like) Henry James – There's something very satisfying about James.

Bax: I always approve of neatness and tidiness. Even in the sea, in the overpowering chaos of the waves, there's always tidiness, there's always a sense of order, and I believe in order. Underlying life, underlying the landscape.

Dilys: I have the image of something – it's not a blueprint, it's like a framework, like a net, but it's not a net. It has a lot of components - (**DG:** Like a soap bubble - Molecular structure)

Bax: Everything has its structure dictated by mathematics. If music has no structure then it is not music as I know it, it is some other kind of sound. I've always liked performers who are orderly. I have no time for the excesses of the personality.

Dilys: I don't suppose he ever knew her, but I've got an image of Jacqueline du Pre, that sort of person, and he didn't care for that type. It was just that style – he didn't like performers of her kind.

Bax: They are too uncontrolled and I do not believe in lack of control.

Dilys: Let me just see if he has any more to say.

Bax: Between us, we will manage it. We've made a good start, I have the basic concept down, we must avoid contamination by sources which would tip the balance into chaotic muddle or overly colourful 'chocolate-box water-colour'. Actually, the 'Celtic Twilight' is interesting. Am I a Celt? I don't know. I don't think that I sound like a Celt. I sound like an Englishman. It was good to see you. We'll talk again. Let me see where I shall take you. We'll go out at night, under the stars, and we will examine the heavens. I will explain to you my thoughts about night and silence.

Dilys: Thank you.

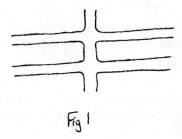

Fig 1

By Frank Borg

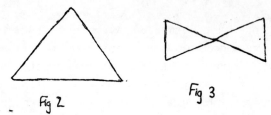

Fig 2   Fig 3

The tree of life
By frank Borg

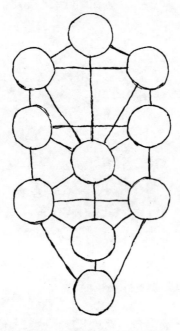

Fig 4

56

6

TRUTH, DARE AND CONSEQUENCES

'Unfortunately, every age has to discover for itself'
Bax

Many of the deeper subtleties of what Bax wanted to convey did not emerge until we had been working for some weeks: he waited, as it were, until we had grown to know each other better. For example, he said in the first 'conversation' that 'the moods shift' so far as night and day were concerned, inferring that he preferred the days. But in later communications he revealed he had experienced periods of depression, and that getting through some days had been like making a long journey towards nightfall and the safety and reassurance of the twilight he seems to have loved.

None of these private, personal details were mentioned on first acquaintance, and we had been in communication for several weeks before we began to appreciate the complexity and urgency of his themes. He revealed in our progressive 'conversations' how he had chosen a way of life that was very different to the easy existence he might have enjoyed as a privileged and moneyed young man. He had made mistakes, undergone personal trials in order to achieve maturity - the same way, he points out to us, that every individual in every generation must do.

'Truth, Dare and Consequences' is the name of a game I remember playing as a child – trivial perhaps, but like many of the insights of childhood, with a directness and honesty that seemed to sum up the essential Bax as he revealed himself to us. As he himself admitted, he never really grew up, never lost that child-like compulsion to find out the truth, to explore and clarify, to take things further. Constantly, he wanted to pit himself against even greater challenges, go to new levels of daring, take extreme risks in order to uncover answers and undergo fresh experience. The results were not always pleasant, sometimes distinctly uncomfortable, but he never rejected the consequences of his mental and physical journeying, trying instead to utilise them positively in his work as part of his development both as a man and an artist.

There can be no doubting the depth and sincerity of his communications, though he refused to commit himself at first, laughing off my enquiries as to why he was undertaking this journey with Paul and myself - 'Don't ask me why - we'll work some reason out between us.' Later, he admitted: 'There is a reason for all this, and I am doing it.' Later still, I realised that right from the start there had been a deep subtext underlying his most seemingly superficial or trivial comments and sometimes he spoke with a clear *diktat*, an emphatic urgency – 'You must tell them', 'This must be said' or 'I want you to write this down'.

With regard to Bax's 'message', he does not have one. He says himself 'We can give nothing to those who come after, and this is perhaps the saddest thing of all.' Yet he adds: 'I can tell you what it was like for me - .' And so this is what he offers us – an account of his own experience, his vision of life and creativity, his personal thoughts.

He is not interested in specifics, being, as he says himself, more concerned with freedom than rigid dogma of any kind. At first, what emerged seemed to be nothing more than a deep concern for a lost way of life and the values this had embodied, reflected in his word-pictures and the images of life in his day - but I soon began to appreciate there was far more here than simple nostalgia.

Whatever his motives, Bax gives us a completely fresh 'take' not just on the concepts of artistic creation but on trying to live life as a human being – and not just in his own time, but in ours too. Without in any way having a particular axe to grind, and with the utmost tact and subtlety, he makes realistic, relevant comments on the problems of today that have the power to pull us up sharp, make us stop, consider and reassess.

He speaks of conductors – critics - 'authority figures' – but we could just as well apply his comments to politicians, even world leaders. Amazingly, he has pertinent light to throw on the East/West conflicts of the present day, on multi-culturalism, terrorism, violence and war. He never mentions Iraq, Iran, Palestine, Afghanistan or any of the other trouble spots by name, yet there are clear indications here of points he has to make regarding the escalating East/West dilemmas of our time.

As I worked on the manuscript, I had begun to select what I considered suitable quotations from literature to lead into each chapter. Finding myself unmistakably directed in the fourth 'conversation' to the famous lines from the *Rubaiyat of Omar Khayyam* - 'Tis all a checker-board of Nights and Days', I had an overwhelming conviction that my other 'quotes' were superfluous, that Bax wanted me to use the *Rubaiyat* as a lead-in to all 'his' chapters. I found that not only did the verses prove extremely appropriate, but certain conclusions were presented for my attention.

The *Rubaiyat* was written in the former Persia (now Iran) in the 11th century, and translated into English by a Victorian scholar, Edward FitzGerald. When the First Edition appeared in 1859, it caused a sensation because the philosophies enshrined within it directly challenged the accepted western beliefs of the day, particularly the church's rigid teachings on life after death. Over a hundred years later, this document has found its own place among some of the most influential ever produced in the west on the nature of life and death.

Eastern philosophies have centuries of historical development behind them, and we are inclined to forget that the western world was still inhabited by primitive tribes when civilization as we know it was beginning to emerge from the areas between the Tigris and the Euphrates. However we in the west choose to regard ourselves now, Bax reminds us in his compelling images of interconnectedness and unity that all are one, that it was the ancient land of Mesopotamia that cradled the wisdom of all our cultures.

Apart from the specific pieces of poetry referred to in the 'conversations', I also found it impossible to ignore the influence of Swinburne, whose philosophies were regarded as just as shocking as those in the *Rubaiyat* when first published.

Though he mentions nothing of any personal belief or religion as such, and has no overt comment to make on the ethics of waging wars, Paul discovered that Bax's family was descended from Quakers, which perhaps speaks for itself. I found it fascinating that he deliberately chose in the *Rubaiyat* such a fluid and eastern text to complement his own very western words. More than that, I was staggered to discover how accurately the *Rubaiyat* reflects and opens up his personal comments, his beliefs and thoughts: he too tells us to live in the moment, to grasp life; and he expresses his overwhelming appreciation, his joy in and thankfulness for sensual pleasures, for the richness of the physical, even while he strives constantly towards the unseen realms of the spirit.

Though Bax admits to no specific faith as such, the *Rubaiyat* is according to Laurence Housman: ' - an elegy on all faiths whatsoever. It states its case with a certain touch of melancholy, but without any cry of distress. Too resigned to be poignant, too philosophical to be bitter about it, it dismisses the dream, and accepts with appetite – almost with gratitude – what is left.'

Bax made no direct comment on any of these topics, but his points had been skilfully made. Paul commented when we discussed how this unexpected turn of events had given us both food for thought: 'He was a very clever man.'

*

He talks of expansion of awareness, of challenge - and his own life seems to have embodied a continual sense of striving and progression. Perhaps one of the characteristics that marked his 'conversations' for me was his courage as well as his humility. He never sat back on his laurels, became complacent or opinionated. He was never tempted to stand still and in his own words, fossilise. He plunged forward, however stormy the seas ahead.

He never avoided the emotional impact of the gulfs that emerged between the ideal and the reality in his own life. Early and romantically emotive connections with Ireland were severed by the shock of confrontation with death and violence in the flesh: his romantic ideal of woman-kind was to be continually shaken, if not actually shattered - yet even in his disillusion he was never afraid to renew and re-enter the beautiful dream.

He illustrates how it can often be a burden to have too much awareness, but the suffering incurred helps us to develop both as artists and human beings. Bax did not try to stave off pain by living in the past. His youthful idealism – particularly regarding the troubles in Ireland - brought him agonies of disillusionment. He was so traumatised that he was never to hold any fanatical view again. He had moved on to awareness of the 'bigger picture', and was still perhaps moving on when he died.

His thoughts on war and conflict became very much his own private property. Awareness was what gave strength and authority to his later compositions, but he did not pronounce

61

publicly, and the points he makes here in the 'conversations' are very much in keeping with this attitude.

Bax has not tried to ignore or avoid difficult subjects or offer bland palliatives. He has recognised and acknowledged the problems that confront us now. His own deeply felt viewpoint is offered, but he does not proselytize or make any attempt to influence individual thought. This is the mark of his greatness and maturity.

7
NIGHT AND SILENCE
In conversation with Bax – 3

Myself when young did eagerly frequent
Doctor and Saint, and heard great Argument
About it and about: but evermore
Came out by the same Door as in I went.

Edward FitzGerald
The Rubaiyat of Omar Khayyam

Dilys: I'm going to focus back in the Night and Silence, that was what he gave me – I do get a sense that he says I've been looking forward to this – he says he's really been looking forward to it. I wanted to tell him that we've been in touch with a potential publisher – and told one or two close friends - He's saying, that doesn't matter, don't get too involved, what matters is doing this -

Dilys: I've got an image of the top of a mountain or a hill somewhere. It's quite peaked so it could well be Scotland – the top of a hill, a mountain peak. As though it's being looked at from the air – I don't know whether he ever went up in an aeroplane – what I've got is more like a glider kind of plane, not an aeroplane, a sort of glider for pleasure – drifting about like a butterfly or something on the air. A lot of chaotic pictures at the moment – I'm trying to get back – I still can't get a coherent picture -

Dilys: I've got the sea again. The sea is more of a connection than the Night and Silence, that will come through later. He's saying, there's always such a pressure of images and ideas to be put across and the pressure is like water building up behind a dam, but often you can't find the right way to let it out. It's the creative process he's talking about as well, the same as I'm trying to find a way to express this and let it through. He's saying, there's such a lot to say, but the channel sometimes doesn't seem to present itself or it seems too narrow, so we're finding a way in, finding the channel -

Bax: The creative process is like the sea. The waves – the surging of the sea.

Dilys: The picture I have at the moment is a sea wall with the sea lapping – the waves coming in against some old stone water steps that are covered in seaweed and barnacles.

Bax: You have to keep the sea back - you have to keep the ideas back. You can't just let things roam. Last time I was talking about form and shape, this time I'm talking about discipline and restraint. The disciplines and techniques that restrain one from squandering. If the sea was allowed to come in, not stopped by the sea wall or by the steps against the wall of the harbour, there would be chaos. There have to be boundaries and there have to be barriers to restrain thoughts and ideas as well.

Dilys: I still have the sea coming in against the sea wall and these steps – I can see only the steps and the sea – focusing very much on them. The small waves coming in against the steps – they're just lapping gently as they come in.

Bax: It's a calm scene with boats riding at anchor – but that tells you nothing of what's going on out on the far deep. It's the edge of the vortex - The deep things go on – the earth-shaking things go on and the ideas, the brilliant ideas and wonderful images build up deep inside the mind - or the ocean, if you're talking about the sea -

Bax: This is an image of creation. It's the creative process for the music -

Bax: You have to try to encompass all of it, you have to encapsulate all of it. You've got to be able to connect or be aware of the great depths where the surges are happening. You don't see them happen, but you see the results as they spread. Sometimes the results are huge crashing storms and waves – great spray -

Dilys: I can see the cliffs now, probably the kind of thing you'd see round Tintagel. Huge storms and crashing waves – - raw energy, destructive. But then the same things are revealing themselves in the slight lapping against the sea steps, which is a beneficial, utilitarian thing. And he's saying, the steps are there to assist you to mount from the sea, to make it easy. The rocks and the great storms don't make it easy for you. The disciplines, the structural disciplines are like steps from the sea, up from the harbour – which is quite deep, because otherwise the boats couldn't be moored there. The depth is there but the steps and the way that they're built help you to climb and pass from the element of sea to the element of land. It's bridging, utility, processes of transition which are necessary in order for things to proceed in an orderly manner. For the ideas as well, if you're talking about the music, to be comprehensible.

Bax: I used to stand on the seashore, I'd stand sometimes in the middle of the storm - by the edge of the shore - I nearly got swept away. Sometimes it was a miracle that the elements didn't take me. I took too many risks. I had to do it because otherwise you don't have that sense of being close enough to

67

the source of it all. I always took risks and I was a fool in some cases. I shouldn't have done it but I did, especially when I was younger. Nobody ever knew about the times when I put myself at actual risk. You don't tell other people about your moments of great foolishness where you're on the verge, teetering on the edge of the abyss and you are nudged back again by nature - the Earth, the world - whatever nudges you back again because you could just as well have fallen the other way -

Bax: I had to take these risks in the music as well, because it's the only way. If you don't reach the boundaries or you don't try to cross them, you never get that sense of the great power that's kept in check.

Dilys: We know he liked the sea – but I don't see him going in for sailing boats and yachting. I don't think he liked that, but I think he was very fascinated by sea voyages. He might have made sea voyages where he was quite comfortable, but he wasn't sort of, down in the bilges or steering the ship - He did like comfort.

Bax: Yes, I always liked comfort. I don't believe in suffering unnecessarily. I was brought up to believe that all had their place and it's necessary for some people's place to be there, to do the work for you. This is a natural order. It's something that is regrettable in many ways but it's very necessary because if we were all equal there would be chaos, the same as if everybody allowed all the notes of the scale to become equal. Then there is no way to produce any coherent sound or coherent structure.

Bax: All artists will tell you the same, they all live close to the edge. If they don't their work will never be any good. There were moments when I was seriously afraid that I had gone

68

too far and those were the moments when I was most in danger of death, when I was most alive. It's not to be recommended, but if it finds you or you know that is your way then that is what you have to do. People thought – later – that what I had written was (to use your popular word) 'tame'. But they had no idea that the taming process is what had resulted from my going too close to the edge.

Dilys: He's laughing now, he's saying this is all rather deep, you didn't expect all this today, but I've been waiting to tell you this. It's almost like, it had to be told.

Bax: It had to be got out of the way because it's been building up the same way as the waves build up, and I have to get a certain amount cleared before I can sit back calmly and rock on the gentle seas.

Paul: He says -

Dilys: He's waiting for you to ask him something, actually. He knows you've got something to ask him and he's waiting. The picture I have in my mind as he's waiting is a gentle sea and a very pleasant sunset, just rocking in a little boat. That's where he is at the moment.

Paul: He just said, he thinks that people thought his work was tame -

Bax: Don't tell me what I think, young man. I have been labelled as 'tame'. We were regarded as the elderly, fossilised – fossils -

Dilys: I have a picture now of fossilised shells, fossils, like I saw a shell on his desk – we've got fossilised shells or coral.

Bax: We were regarded as ancient when modern took over. Admit it. You never regarded me as a great innovator, and you have never regarded me as an exciting and thrilling composer of works which transported you to the edges of infinity.

Dilys: He's laughing now, at you.

Paul: Well that was probably my impression some years ago, apart from the work that almost everybody knows, *Tintagel*, but the other works, as opposed to being 'tame', as people thought they were, I find - I now find, myself – I'm discovering that they are very exciting. Not always -

Dilys: He's interrupting now.

Bax: You have discovered some discrimination, but far too many of the so-called -

Dilys: I've got him talking in inverted commas, he's saying far too many of the so-called, not 'intelligentsia', the word he's using is like 'enlightened' - I can't tell what the word is, it's a word in inverted commas like 'critic' or 'intelligentsia' or something, but that's not the word he's using. Far too many of these so-called wise -

Paul: Acres?

Dilys: No, not quite. He's talking about music critics I think - whatever he would have called them. He may have called them something in his work, you might find it in his autobiography, but I can't get the word exactly. He's saying, far too many of them are far too focused on their own interpretations or their own opinions.

Bax: They were not composers. They could not write music. They did not go to the edge. They sit there in the theatre boxes -

Dilys: I've got plush boxes – the Albert Hall or somewhere like that in my mind.

Bax: - They sit there and explain, and expound. Only the ones who play, the musicians – the true musicians – the true strugglers with the disciplines – are there on the edge, and they know what it's like to be on the edge - But I suppose they are necessary. This is the way it is. This is the way of the world. But nobody is going to shut me in my grave and they're not going to shut me in my grave as an old grey-beard. I fully intend to rise up like a -

Dilys: I've got a picture of a water-spout, a tornado or a water-spout.

Bax: - and sweep across the complacency of the established order. Yes. Young man, don't worry about your words, follow your head and heart. You are falling over your words, you're tripping on them with your tongue. If you had the discipline to sing, you would realise that everything has to come smoothly. One does not allow proprieties to stand in the way of the true notes. The notes – the sounds – what is being said and communicated is what matters, not whether it is appropriate to say it. I've lived longer than you – a lot longer – I know what you are trying to say, I know what you think. Give me credit for having some insight into your appreciation of my work.

Dilys: He's laughing, really, he's laughing.

Bax: I think you have great potential. I feel you may go far. But don't give me your clever padded-seat questions – ask with your heart, speak with your soul.

Paul: Well! I find, going back to this comment he made about some people thinking that his work was 'tame'. I feel personally that his musical language is not straightforward.

Bax: Why should it be?

Paul: Exactly.

Bax: Who is to judge these things? Who is to say which language one should speak in? I speak in my own language, and the language that I speak in was learnt on the peak of the mountain, on the edge of the world. If I could have fallen off the edge of the world, I would have done it and I went to the very edge. In many ways, I put myself in the hands of the almighty -

Dilys: I think this might have something to do with a shipwreck – not a real shipwreck, but an experience, something that very much affected him, to do with being in danger. It's very much this thing about being on a boat, and going to the edge of the world - I don't know in what respect – symbolically, even - it seems something to do with being in danger of dying. I think he was, at one time certainly – more than one time perhaps – very close to dying, and this wasn't in the war, or in the bombing. It was something he did, or went to or knew.

Bax: Yes, I lived there, and then when you have lived those moments, all the rest is shallow and in its way meaningless. And yet, we need it because you could not live on the peaks – you could not survive – it would be too – too -

Dilys: Agh! Words again. It would be too - I've got a picture of a word that means tearing – tearing apart - I can't think of the right word. He's saying he doesn't really care what they think anyway.

Bax: The trouble with dying is that you become dismissed as 'dead'.

Dilys: Again, he's laughing.

Bax: When you are dead, your work has no chance to develop further. It then passes into the hands of cataloguists (**DG**: That was the word he used) and compilers who file it away, in my case under B for Bax. And so now my work lives in files under B for Bax. Where are the companions who will come with me to the edge of the world? Some of them are playing in orchestras.

Dilys: I have a picture of an orchestra playing – particularly a big French horn – seems to be important – and all of them scraping away with their violins or whatever.

Bax: Under the stage they sweat and they squirm and scrape with their eyes focused on a very small area and their fingers feeling the stops. Their attention is so focused. That is their tiny world, the notes on the page and the music they're playing. It's not necessarily the conductor who takes them on the journey. There were some terrible conductors.

Dilys: He didn't have a great deal of time for conductors, I don't think. Certainly not all of them. - He had a terrific sense of humour.

Bax: Too many conductors have very solemn faces. They should be going into the orchestra with a whip, whipping

73

them into a frenzy. How can you send them to the edge of the world when you're sitting there with a long, hang-dog, important face? Once they become conductors – as with people in authority, often – they become confined, their position restricts them from taking those journeys themselves. Many conductors would like to, but because of the accepted ways, they are not allowed to. They stand on the podium and they wave their white stick. They are the blind sometimes, leading the sightless.

Dilys: I don't think he liked some conductors or orchestras at all! Do you want to say any more about the 'tame' music, Paul?

Paul: Well, my observation is that if a composer's style is not straightforward, it is difficult and demands attention -

Dilys: He's interrupting again – he knows what you are saying.

Bax: But how should one find a way into these difficult areas if you do not actually struggle and strive? If you're going into a jungle, there's no path.

Paul: Exactly.

Bax: What is the use of a person who stands there and tells one what to do and points with a white stick? They should be leading the troops at the front and far too many of those in authority -

Dilys: I think he's talking not just about conductors, but everybody – this is applying it to life.

Bax: Far too many of people in authority have forgotten what it is like to lead from the front. They have forgotten what it's like to be trying to beat a way through the jungle with no knowledge of where you are going.

Paul: Yes, for a lot of people a work of pretty tunes – tunes easy to follow – they can misinterpret as a wonderful work.

Bax: Pretty tunes of all kinds have always had their place.

Dilys: I think he must have written some pretty tunes for the piano himself – easy, or just tuneful.

Bax: They have their place. Pretty tunes have always had their place, But no chocolate-box picture - (**DG**: I had an image of a 'chocolate-box' kind of village, thatched cottages, etc) – no chocolate-box picture will satisfy the soul that yearns for the edges of the world. I was never satisfied not to know. The edges of the world are not a comfortable place. They are not for everyone. We are talking here to the ones who yearn for them, not for those who wish to sit and shake their baby rattles.

Dilys: I have a picture of babies' rattles with bells on. That's the little pretty tunes.

Bax: For infants, that is all that they can do. They shake the rattle and they say: 'What a wonderful sound this makes. What a pretty tune.' But the struggler and striver for the darker, the deeper communications with the gods, cannot stay at home and watch the baby shaking his rattle and smile. He has to go to the edges of the world and find what lies there or beyond. I have to do it. It is something that is in you. It is in you or it isn't in you. If it is in you, then you do it. Perhaps you become a musician, perhaps you become an artist. You

75

learn the disciplines, you learn the boundaries and the restraints. You learn the bridges. You follow all the routes, you follow all the paths there are, you make maps for those to follow you. You try your best. You have to strive -

Bax: The babies and the infants are in their bassinets. They sit in their little lacy bonnets and shake their rattles, and with them to some extent, the future lies because they will grow. But how can they grow if those who must find a way for them have never been, or discovered the way? How can they be protected? How can they be nurtured? When I was alive, I didn't think much of the future. I did not consider the future. I was too concerned with the moment and to some extent one has to do that, but now I can see that the future is all that matters. The moment is the tool one has, but the future is the ultimate aim.

Dilys: Although it's serious. he's laughing now, he's laughing again and saying don't ask me to explain this because I cannot.

Bax: When I was on the edge of the world, then yes, I understood all in a flash of lightning or a crash of thunder. It all came and I tried to put this into my work. I tried to put the voice of the storm and the voices of the elements. I tried to put the knowledge into what I wrote down but it's very, very much of an echo. And for the children sitting at home in their nursery with their bells – their little bells and rattles – there is very little to give them -

Bax: We all tried in our way. I personally have always travelled alone. One can talk to others about the experience – one can exchange experiences, but how do we know – how did I know – whether another artist had travelled to the same edge of the world that I had? The more you exchange experiences with others, the less sure you become that they understand what you are saying. The more artists come together and discuss their work and their vision, the more one becomes aware that those visions are very disparate. If one has seen an angel, the angel may be the same angel, and yet take a different form. Everything is very much to do with my own journey, my own travelling alone, and no-one could come with me.

Dilys: I don't know whether he had grand-children – babies in the family. These weren't his own children, they were later on, very young babies, children sitting in cots and prams with little bonnets on, rattling their rattles. I feel he might have had some children that he was particularly focused on – even children in an orphanage or somewhere he went later where he saw them. He's very concerned with this vision of the future for the children – not so much in a personal way, but more like looking at a generation and saying: These are the unaware young souls.

Bax: I thought of writing music for the souls. But the music that I wrote when I was alive has no place in the nursery of the souls. They must learn their own music. They must find their own music.

Paul: Their own level?

Dilys: Their own music - I have now an image of fireworks in the night sky, some kind of fireworks. We come now to the night – the Night and Silence.

Bax: The night is not silent. The night is filled with sounds and shrieks and death, pain and tragedy. Whether it is the burning of a city over the horizon -

Dilys: I actually think I've got more of a picture of the Vikings, to do with celebrations – fireworks that might have been one of those celebrations of the Vikings somewhere in Scotland (**DG**: 'Up-Helly-Aa') – but he's seeing them as raiders.

Bax: There are always the burning cities over the horizon – the threats from the sea. The same as the night is not silent, then neither is the sea empty. The empty sea, like the dark quiet night, is filled with threats. I wanted to put this into a work - (he might have even done it, Paul) – I wanted to capture this because there is never an easy way, there is always a dark way, a shadow that walks with you and follows you.

Dilys: Again, I feel as though this might be to do with when he was depressed, something he felt very strongly.

Bax: In any work there must be a dark shadow that travels with it, because without a shadow you have no validity.

Dilys: The Shadow - I have Jung – the psychiatrist – and I think he was interested in the work of Jung, because of the spiritual dimension of it. He's talking about the Shadow.

Bax: I felt that before he (Jung) even thought of the concept (of the Shadow) it was there. You can find it in great works of art. There is always that dark side, that down side and it has to be there. It's only through the small things – the steps up from the sea – and keeping the great surging tides at bay, that one can cope. Then you have a secure place for your foot to stand, where you can peer into the dark as well as reach upwards to the heights. Yes, in some ways perhaps, music has to be 'tame', because how can it be otherwise? You can't have it breaking over you like a great crashing wave into the orchestra pit.

Dilys: He's laughing now, he's sort of imagining the orchestra pit filling up with water as the waves come crashing in, and all the people playing their instruments are getting up and running out in a hurry because they're getting flooded out.

Bax: Maybe that is where the authority and the conductors are necessary, because in their very ordinariness they are the everyday, the touchstone, the focus that keeps the great seas from crashing too much in. I find this very fascinating, exploring. I often criticise people for being too ordinary but of course, without the ordinary, without the unimaginative, the boring and the plain and the frustrating restrictions of such establishments and figures, there would be nothing. It is the same with people.

Dilys: He's thinking about the women now, his wife and the woman – or women - that he loved.

Bax: How can one reach the end of the world and sit on the edge of the world, and at the same time sit and watch the children in the bassinet? It was very difficult for me. I found women a great inspiration. The beauty and the wonder of the women I knew, I will always be utterly grateful for, with all my heart, that they were there. But in one way my journey as an artist – an explorer – took me to all the different points of the compass and no-one could come with me - and so they were left behind.

Dilys: I think he felt the women in his life were very much there for him to return to, rather than take with him. Maybe it was his own home and children earlier, because I have this picture now of a wife and children and a home.

Bax: For one of them – to return to - for sustenance, as in bread and water. The other - (**DG:** I have the woman at the piano here) – it was sustenance as in champagne and caviar.

Dilys: He's laughing again.

Bax: But would either of them have been flattered at that description of themselves? I realise that I only touched one tiny facet of the diamond, and that is all one can do. You cannot touch two diamonds and cut, and they can only touch facet to facet. The diamonds cannot meet and become fused on every facet and so there is so much of me that was unknown to these women, and so much of them that was unknown to me. However I yearned – or however they yearned - the rest was not possible. I tried to convey this too in my music.

Paul: Can I ask a personal question?

Bax: I don't promise to answer, young man.

Paul: Did the relationship with Harriet Cohen, the pianist, mean more to him than his wife meant to him, after 1915? Or was the relationship merely spasmodic?

Bax: I have told you how it was. At any time, think of the diamond. They were both diamonds. At any time, a precious stone will sparkle as the light touches it and each one, in their way, the light touched at different times. Each in their way meant to me deep sustenance. I did not speak about it – I could not speak about this. But I never forgot.

Dilys: I have that vision of the house and family, his wife and children.

Bax: It was something that was just as real to me whether the light was touching the relationship – the diamond – or not. It varies according to circumstances and mood and what is needed at any time. Each in their way mattered to me - and other jewels along the way may have been also touched by the light. I was very, very fortunate and very blessed that I was not left to struggle alone. The women that I knew were true diamonds.

Dilys: I'm asking him, shall we stop now, is he satisfied.

Bax: I want you to put this down, that the women in my life were true diamonds, through and through. I will always be grateful for that. Now go – and get on with what has to be done. Lots more to do, and I will be looking forward to our next meeting.

Dilys: I have a hotel, some kind of hotel for our next meeting.

Bax: We will meet at the inn.

Dilys: Thank you.

8

BAX AND WOMEN
Paul Gater

*'I was very, very fortunate and very blessed that I was not left
to struggle alone.'*
Bax

During my research into his life, I failed to come across any
hint of snobbery in Bax's character. He was likeable, witty and
generous. Being of private financial means meant that he
could indulge in anything that took his fancy, but his music
always came first. He worked very hard at it, and as a student
at the Royal Academy of Music during the early 1900s,
astounded his professors with his ability to sight-read, being
able to play straight onto the piano whatever orchestral score
was placed before him – all of which bode well for him in his
career.

Always very attractive and attracted to women, he
encountered many young ladies at the RAM where, it is said,
he had numerous affairs. Myra Hess and Irene Scharrer, both
to become famous pianists, were fellow students he described
at the time as 'very small and eternally giggling.' Another
student – Rebecca Clarke – thought Arnold Bax the most
attractive male student at the establishment in his pale
greenish suit with a carnation in his buttonhole.

March 1918 saw the final break between Bax and his
highly-strung wife Elsita. This had not come lightly to either.
Elsita had been distressingly aware for several years that her
husband was attracted to the young Harriet Cohen while Bax,
meanwhile, had genuinely anguished between duty to his wife
and two children and a deep yearning for freedom of

expression through his art, via the woman to whom he now felt totally drawn. Ultimately, hurt and embittered, Elsita took the children to live with Bax's parents in Cavendish Square.

In June, on the death of Bax's father, Elsita removed with her young family to Golders Green. She never considered divorcing her husband, hoping that some day he might eventually return from his 'wanderings'. But this was never to be, although as his wife and children, they would always receive his financial support.

On quitting their house in Beaconsfield, Bax established himself in comfortable rooms in Hampstead, where he was to stay until the Second World War. The lifestyle suited him, for he never outgrew certain aspects of his adolescence completely, particularly where women were concerned. Absorbed in Irish mythology and poetry, he continually sought the illusive female form – the child-like nymph, brimming with innocence and potential sexuality.

Possibly the most significant woman in his life to embody this dream would be the young pianist Harriet Cohen who, born in London to musical parents, won a scholarship at 12 to the Royal Academy of Music. She was 17 when Bax first saw her in 1913 – shy, slim and petite - in the audience at a concert in the Queen's Hall. Soon she was included in his circle of friends and it was because of his growing obsession with his 'stray from the faery hills' that he postponed a second visit to Ireland the following year. Their relationship deepening, he wrote a number of short piano pieces which he dedicated to 'Tania', as she was known to her intimates. And though nymphs mature - Harriet being no exception - she continued to cast her 'spell' on Bax in different ways for the rest of his life.

By the mid 1920s, he felt that both the quantity and quality of his compositions were on a downward spiral. To his friends he was still very much the charming man they had always known, but in actuality he was deeply depressed. The inevitable disillusionment had set in with regard to Harriet who, though continuing to loyally promote his music and perform his works for the piano, in many ways now domineered him to the point of criticising some of the friends he cultivated within the profession (though she herself was not popular with everyone) and even decreeing which instruments he should or should not compose for.

Quietly yet stubbornly, Bax would hold his ground - horrendous rows resulted, which shattered them both. Physically though, Harriet was delicate and often ill. By 1925, her health and reason worsening, he took her to Switzerland in search of a cure for tuberculosis – not a successful visit as far as their relationship was concerned. Emotionally exhausted, Bax decided on their return home that it was time to distance himself from Harriet, although professionally they would still work together. Perhaps as an obvious over-reaction, he plunged into being 'just one of the boys' for a time, staying with some male musician friends in a rented cottage at Eynsford in Kent.

Weekdays were devoted to music and serious composition, but their weekends were dedicated to playing schoolboy pranks on each other and getting very drunk at the local alehouse. Commentators believe it was during this period that Bax began seriously to cultivate his intake of whisky - something that was to increase considerably in future years. Dilys and I had no idea he had had a drink problem, though in the following 'conversation' he did actually reveal the fact that he liked a 'stiff drink'.

Whilst staying at Eynsford, Bax met Mary Gleaves, an attractive 23 year old woman almost half his age. Though it would be another year (1927) before they would meet again, he was charmed by her, their friendship blossoming during summer afternoons spent rowing on the Thames at Marlow. After the death of her parents Bax (who had with characteristic generosity paid for her father's care) realised just how greatly he was attracted to her. An over-sensitive awareness of the age gap between them warned him not to allow infatuation to overcome common sense in a man of his years – but going by the letters he was soon writing to her while staying in Glencolumcille, a village in West Donegal he had discovered some years before as his spiritual haven, it was obvious that Bax was in love with her. His mythical nymph had materialised once more. Back in England he wrote to her again, this time in flowing, flowery epithets, and by December of that year (1929) she had his full commitment, although he did not introduce her to his friends.

Despite their happiness together, Bax still felt torn between the real and materialistic post World War One and Irish Civil War world, and his fine dream-world of legend. The images of his fantasies - included the mythical Tir na nOg, island of eternal youth lying in the west beyond the sunset – held him so fast he would never entirely escape from them. But though this conflict was never resolved within him, for the rest of his life Mary would always be at hand, her presence soothing, comforting and offering solace.

The following year was a very happy one for them both. Now he was a real star and performances of his music had become major, and frequent, events. 'Things northern' having by now also captured his imagination - the music of Sibelius in particular – Bax went up alone during the winter of 1929 to Morar in Inverness-shire, on the West Coast of Scotland where, staying at the Station Hotel, he completed his *Third Symphony*.

His compositions throughout the next decade or so (particularly most of the symphonies) were roughed out in London and orchestrated elsewhere – usually at Morar. After 1929, generally in the winter, Mary was to go with him: away from the professional and social demands of London, he could work on his scores and both he and Mary could enjoy the wild and wintry glories of the Scottish west coast.

The 1930s saw Bax a much less prolific composer as he became plagued by his 'black shadow' – his depression – and his confidence in composition began to wane. We were fascinated to discover that Dilys's early suspicions and Bax's later communications to us in the 'conversations' about depression turned out to be so very accurate. His solace, of course, was Mary, still his 'secret love' even though often, going abroad on holiday with friends, he would leave her at home.

There was a very private side to Bax. In the eyes of his travelling companions he was lively, entertaining company. From his letters to Mary, however, it appears that he was far from enjoying his travels, feeling miserably alone, longing to be with her. For whatever reason though, she was kept very much in the background. When attending public functions, or if invited out to dinner by friends, Bax often chose to take Harriet with him – their names being still linked in the eyes of most of their friends and the public. Mary represented the most secret and deeply hidden area of his life.

Bax received news that Natalia Skarginski, the young Ukrainian woman who had rejected his proposal of marriage in 1910, had been badly treated by the man she had chosen instead, and was now in ill health, living in poverty with her daughter. Typically, the composer sent money to help her but in 1934, he heard via a letter written in English from a friend that Natalia, weakened by lack of food in the grimness of those times, had died. Once again reality had crushed the beautiful dreams of earlier optimism and youth.

For Bax though, life and love continued to entice. In 1937, while staying with his friends, the Irish-German musician Aloys Fleischmann and his wife Tilly in a rented cottage in Bantray Bay, he was to meet Anne Crowley, a wonderful Irish woman with whom he felt he had so much in common. They struck up a correspondence (in Gaelic, which Bax had taught himself) and met up whenever he was in

Dublin. In November of the same year he also encountered Christine Ryan, another young woman half his age who he felt swept him up into a world of romantic fantasy. The infatuated letters he wrote to her were once again those of an adolescent, though caution prevailed as Bax decided to 'dampen down' the relationship. They did, however, continue to write to each other well into the years of World War Two.

In 1947, again while staying with the Fleischmanns – this time in Cork – Bax heard that his wife, Elsita, had died. He had continued to provide for her throughout her life, and had also provided houses for both Harriet and Mary, and bought Harriet a mews flat she used as a studio.

He chose to say nothing to Harriet of Elsita's death, though they still saw each other on a professional basis, and she only discovered the news the following September while involved in recording the Suite Bax had arranged from the music he had composed for the film *Oliver Twist*. Suddenly it was made public - Elsita's will was published.

Harriet, now assuming the way was open for marriage and for her to become Lady Bax, confronted the composer, and a dreadful scene ensued. She was staggered to be informed that if there *was* to be another Lady Bax, it would not be her but Mary Gleaves – of whom she had never heard mention.

In the event, Bax never remarried.

9

AT THE HOLIDAY HOTEL
In conversation with Bax – 4

Tis all a checker-board of nights and days
Where Destiny for men with pieces plays
Hither and thither moves and mates and slays
And one by one back in the closet lays

Edward FitzGerald
The Rubaiyat of Omar Khayaam

Dilys: He gave me an inn, a holiday hotel or pub - might be the same place as that courtyard was, with the paved yard - I can't get him yet, he's not there - images like postcards or photographs in a book, an album - very much like he said, that his music was the album, it was a journey through the places that he loved - and a lot of places that he didn't like so much - I'm just sort of trying to get a connection -

Paul: Is this the Station Hotel in Morar? (**DG**: Identified in his research as the place where Bax used to stay)

Dilys: I think it's a hotel where he lived or stayed. I think it's somewhere up on the west coast – could be of Scotland – I don't know if it's the Station Hotel, but it's a place he stayed. He said: I'll meet you at the hotel, the holiday pub or inn. The feeling I've got for today is a sadder feeling than before, it's not so much a lot of pressure like the sea, it's more sombre. This is his voice now, very quiet.

Bax: There are some things that one approaches reluctantly. Last time I was talking about the Shadow – we were talking about the Shadow. This Shadow is not an easy part of living, but it has to be there. This is not easy for me. I want to talk about or go into areas that perhaps will revive pain or suffering of some kind. On the surface I was a - quote - 'laugh a minute'. People didn't regard me as a sad or sombre man but regarding the depressions and the glooms (previously mentioned), there are parts of one's life or one's existence – parts of one's world – that are places where no-one sees and you don't want them to see.

Dilys: Why have we got this suddenly when I thought it was going to be so pleasant – at the holiday hotel?

Bax: In a way, everything turns upside down.

Dily: I'm looking now at some music chords (written down).

Bax: Between the minor chords and the major chords there is very little difference, but it can be a huge difference in effect or intensity.

Dilys: I have him now much younger, perhaps when he first learned music – maybe even under 10 – a youngish lad, where he was actually learning, on the piano - again, I think he must have learned on the piano – the first time that he ever realised -

Bax: I had a revelation, when I played a sharp and a natural and realised that the sound changed. It was almost as though a door opened, a key turned in the lock and a door opened. I realised then how the notes – the keys - are so subtly different but the difference can be immense. The same thing is in life.

Some things can be so little but they can wipe out the colour in the world and change it, they take away all one's strength.

Dilys: I don't know what happened to him, but something did which gave him this feeling, this sense that he'd lost everything, or everything had changed. It's to do I think with this place where he was, or where he suddenly got a revelation – which I think was somewhere up in the north? - a sort of wild countryside. Not quite by the sea, because he wasn't exactly on the sea's edge, but a bit inland. There are mountains there as well. (**DG**: Could this have been Natalia's rejection of him in the Ukraine?)

Bax: My paintbox was the music and my paints were the notes, the ink with which I filled in the notes on the paper.

Dilys: Filling in the notes on the staves, I can see black ink notes being filled in.

Bax: In many ways we need our tools – our particular tools - because when we lose our way, the only things that we can hold onto to see us through this difficult territory are the familiar tools we use. Sometimes the tools might not be what they appear. In my case it was the pen and ink that wrote down the notes, they made sense for me and saw me through. Some fogs or clouds or glooms can be so dark that you think you are never going to come through them. This was a very private part that people didn't see. Maybe we all need this. I wonder sometimes whether perhaps we need to suffer in this way because if we didn't, we wouldn't be forced to find our way, forced to discover the tools - the threads – the ropes - that will see us through.

Dilys: I've got an image of a huge trackless moor or plain. Or even classically, the thread that sees the spirit through the labyrinth – in the story of the Minotaur, Theseus and Ariadne with the thread in the maze.

Bax: Mazes are very interesting. I have personally always found mazes and labyrinths very fascinating. And puzzles. I like the puzzles where one has to find one's way. In a way, music does this. In a way we do it all the time. We're always faced (with it). Each day is a trackless waste and each day we have to choose the thread that we will follow to bring us through to the evening, safely to the night, from dawn till nightfall. Sometimes the labyrinth can seem very like an open plain.

Dilys: I have again similar pictures of flat scrubland with hills, rocky. I'm seeing more like an open plain with some rock, but it's quite open. This is the image he's using to illustrate. The labyrinth can sometimes appear as an open plain or open moor with no restrictions, no points of reference at all. Sometimes it's just as difficult to know the way through a completely open, unconfined freedom as it is to try to find one's way through a very constricting and narrow passage.

Bax: Sometimes we see even less when we're in a wide space with the sky above, and to get through a day can sometimes be more difficult in an open space – on open moorland. It can be more difficult to find a safe way through that to the evening, than to try to fight one's way out of a labyrinth. Different people's – different artists' versions of labyrinths will differ. Different versions of labyrinths are like mouse-holes. To a mouse, the mouse-hole is a doorway into the wider world, to freedom, but to the cat which is watching the mouse-hole, it is a trap. It's the same with labyrinths and mazes.

Dilys: I don't think he is interested in what other people did, how they saw things.

Bax: What does it matter what I think? My thought, my impression, is of no relevance. You will see and take from it – each one - what you want or what you find in it. If I didn't know it when I was young, perhaps the one piece of wisdom I have learned is that one's opinion of what others do or create – as their works of art – will be entirely superfluous, since they will see their works of art as 'works of art', whereas I may see it as a delusion or a snare or even a trap, as the cat watching the mouse-hole. The mouse creates the outside world in its imagination. He creates a world in beautiful glowing colours, and he goes through the mouse-hole into that world. The cat inhabits a different world. Each in their way is right, and what links their realities is the actual mouse-hole itself, the gateway. Gateways as well as mazes – gateways may be the same gateways, but the gateway may take us from any point of the compass to any other, and how can we judge or know which aspect of the gateway is being entered by any other person, and passing through to where?

Dilys: He's saying this is like a knot.

Bax: I don't find this is a profitable exercise, about other people's perceptions, because I can only speak about my own. I can only tell you about my efforts to follow the path that I followed through those long open moorlands and empty days, and between one bar of music and the next. When you think about it, science in its way tells us a lot, but in fact art tells us more. If you look at two bars of music, you are jumping perhaps from one universe to another between one bar and another, if there is a change of key. You can leap from one planet – or one galaxy, even, to another. This is what I find fascinating, the immensity of the small, as it were. A natural, or a sharp added to music, and suddenly you have created a world of chaos. This is what I found so interesting in the sea, because the sea does this. It's there, it's always moving yet it goes nowhere, and yet the very variations of every mood and every thing are encompassed in the sea -

Bax: We come from the sea, everything comes from the sea. I used to think this when I stood and watched the waves, and I wondered sometimes, were the waves throwing us out, were we being rejected to the land? Was life being rejected and thrown out from the waters, and are we actually the rejects from some great immensity, that we're not perfect and we must perfect ourselves? Or were we thrown out because we were finished, as it were, because we could then carry out (some unspecified task). I don't know, it becomes very confusing, but I feel that in many ways, the secrets are in the sea. That was why I wrote about the sea. All things in their way (lead to the sea) – all tracks lead across the moor, all the days lead to night but all nights lead to the sea. All leads back to the sea. I have always turned to the west. I've always turned to the sunset. The dawns marked days of work, a struggle and an effort. The dawns marked the work of preparing for the trek through to nightfall. The nights were the times of promise, the places where things were known.

Dilys: I have this picture again of him playing the piano as it was going dark.

Bax: Sometimes that was all that saved me. Knowing the night would come.

(long pause)

Bax: Let me tell you about some of the journeys. I also journeyed through areas where there (were) cornfields –

96

golden cornfields with poppies. Again, I thought of the tiny creatures hidden below the corn. To me, the cornfields waved and moved in the breeze like a sea, but underneath that sea, the little tiny creatures were living lives unknown to me. Even if I had managed to part the corn and find them, I can never enter their lives. I felt very much the restrictions, only the music helped me to bridge it -

Bax: This was something that was personal, it was private. But perhaps to some extent we all feel it. I felt that I wanted to know everything, I felt that I wanted to reach for the sky and the stars and the universe, I wanted to encompass the sea and understand. Sometimes I felt I would die from the longing to get outside of my skin and my body and actually melt – or meld – into the great reality that was there. It wasn't a comfortable thing, and I did not enjoy it. It was this difficult and dark side that drove me, almost one wanted to leap off those edges of the world just to put the torment to rest. This was a torment that drove me. Music or creation, or even finding out or knowing oneself, it's not an easy master, not an easy way to go. It is something that can drive you unbearably, so that you can't stand the longing and the frustration.

Bax: Of course, not all my days were like this, but I want to tell you about these because they are in a way like the chessboard. There are black squares and white squares and although the black pawns walk on the black squares and the white pawns walk on the white squares, in fact this is not so. We all cross the checker-board all the time and we walk in the white squares and the black squares. We are never going to know which one is coming or which way we will go. All of them look the same. You never know on a chessboard, where is the end. You never know where you are heading, because beyond a black and a white square is just another black and a white square. This is why we need the tools and we need the threads that will see us safely through the confusions and the bewilderments - There was a time when I was ill.

Dilys: I don't know what kind of illness – confined to bed, I think. If it wasn't war or a wound, it was some time when he had a delirium, some sort of delirium.

Bax: There was a time when I lay between the black and the white squares - (pause)

Dilys: I think he's lost the thread.

Bax: Yes, it is so difficult, one loses one's way. In thoughts like these, the only things that will keep one (safe) is not to worry about where one is going but to hold on to the tools one has and trust those tools will see you through. There isn't any shape anyway. There isn't any shape at all. When I was in this experience I could see that there was nothing, and I hung like something on a thread, between black and white and dark and light. I had no way of telling whether I was dead or alive, or whether I was in light or darkness. In many ways this was the most salutary experience of my life. It taught me that nothing can be measured and so the measures that we make, whether they are the bar-lines on the music or whether they are the ropes that tie us together as we are crossing dangerous terrain, we simply have to rely on them, that they will somehow hold us up and bring us through.

Bax: I feel this must be said. This must be said. I want you to say this very strongly. There is no way, there is no answer, there are no rules. There is nothing by which to measure the immensity, and so, do not try. Simply take what you have been given, the tools that you have, the threads, the ways to guide you, and hold onto those and go forward.

Dilys: I'm asking him now about whether this is something like a faith, or a philosophy – whether a faith would do this.

Bax: Whichever. Whatever the tools are called, they are all the same. They give you something to hold and they give you a line or a thread of sorts to follow.

Dilys: I don't know whether he has any opinion on faith.

Bax: My faith to me was something very blinding that came – it was a bit like flames from Mount Sinai, an incredible revelation.

Paul: Was this the revelation he had when he was twelve?

Dilys: I don't know what his age was, but he saying it was a revelation. He had all these things coming in a revelation.

Bax: I've told you about the delirium and I've told you about the loss. I had lost my way, and the revelations came. Sometimes, when one has received a revelation – when one has received some kind of vision - one cannot put it into a perspective of time, because revelations are not part of time. They put one outside of time - and who is to say when the revelation happened? You only know that it happened and you have experienced it, but exactly when or how, you may never be able to say. Sometimes the revelations appear to have come, but you can't pin them down. The same as with inspiration. You can't pin down inspiration and say that it came on such a day.

Dilys: I think it was when he was young. If you could find when he was ill, or had this delirium – or when he got lost.

Bax: So many times in one's life, you stand on another edge of the world, so the revelations can't be quantified. The same as the immensities can't be measured. One thing I will tell you is that if you look for revelations, they will not come. Many a time I walked through the day – followed the road across the moor. I went and I looked for them, I searched for them.

Dilys: I think this is Scotland, the moorlands there. This must be why he went to Scotland.

Bax: I thought I would find them there. But they came when I was nowhere near a revelation, and how it happened, I don't know. I just knew that somewhere I had had it.

Dilys: I have a picture of a railway station, with steam engines, a large terminus where he might have caught the train up to Scotland.

Bax: Perhaps it was even a moment in the steam of the station. The steam blots out – clouds of steam in a railway station can surround one - and between one breath and the next, you have had a revelation. You can't tell people how or why. You have simply had a revelation, and that is that. Try not to pin things down in so many words. There are some things that are impossible to quantify or describe, and a revelation is one of them.

Paul: I think that is put very succinctly. I can say the same. I have had revelations when least expected, but if I have gone looking for them, they have never been there.

Bax: Young man, you will go further than you think, if you stop thinking about going further.

Dilys: He's smiling.

100

Paul: (laughing) So am I.

Bax: Sometimes one cannot explain to those who seek and ask for you to share your wisdom and experience. How can the cat and the mouse converse? My wisdom is either cat wisdom or mouse wisdom – and I don't know which it is. All I know is that whoever may be asking me to share it could be the opposite, perhaps I am cat and they are mouse, perhaps I am mouse and they are cat. I might try to share it, but perhaps by doing so I am destroying the thing I seek to preserve. I can only tell you to use the tools you have -

Bax: I tried to put this in my music. It was impossible, because I can work – I can conjure - with words, but words cannot convey. You need a deeper method, for me it was the music. But even the music is limited. What would the notes on the page mean to someone who cannot read them? What would the sounds mean to someone who is deaf? The frustration can be so terrible it can destroy you, and here is where these small tools – the little tool – the thread in your hand, is all that you have to bring you through. You don't have a rescue party, you don't have some great rope or strong cord. You have a tiny thread, and that is all there is. But think of the strength of a spider web. Something held me up when I was there suspended in the void, and I don't know what it was, but it was immensely strong. The strength was something that defied the power of the universe. So one does not ask. One holds onto that thread and moves forward, heading for the west and the twilight, the ending of the day.

Dilys: I'm asking whether this is what he had to tell us on this occasion, because I felt there were so many things he wanted to say.

Bax: Perhaps I haven't made it clear, but the more I have to tell you – the more I want to say – the less I am able to. In many ways, I am afraid even to try. We can give nothing to those who come after, and this is perhaps the saddest thing of all. I can tell you about what it was like for me – and so can anyone who was there – but it's like the wind whistling across this open moorland. No-one will hear it and no-one will understand it. Each in your way must follow the path of your own.

Dilys: I am asking, did he always feel so sad, like this?

Bax: One never appreciates, when you know that you are omnipotent and can conquer the world, especially the young. It would never occur to you to be sad. The sadness comes as one becomes perhaps older and wiser. With wisdom comes a great awareness of the futility of it all. Maybe I am passing to a phase beyond this one, where I will begin to see things in another light, and where this will all make sense. I am going through a black square on the chequer-board and beyond this there is going to be one of such white, bright light that I can't even imagine it. In fact, they never really stop, because we all pass through a black and a white square following each other, and there is no end to the chess-board. There is no boundary, or at least, I haven't seen it yet. In one way this can seem depressing – and this is why we need the little rituals, the little barriers and boundaries we create ourselves. I feel that music has been the thread – the small thread – that has upheld me, and it will do so, as it upholds the birds. The bird sings, creates music without knowing what it is doing. It is weaving magic.

Dilys: He's laughing now.

Bax: Again, don't ask me to explain all this, because I cannot. I know so little. But today it was a black square that I wanted you to walk with me. I wanted to share with you what I could to help to ease that lack of hope and that lack of purpose. It is a terrible thing, to be lost on a black square, but as long as you hold onto the thread you will never lose your way entirely. Now, let us be more cheerful. We are in the holiday hotel – and this was why I asked you to meet me here. I knew I was going to need a stiff drink after all that.

Dilys: I have him going into a bar.

Bax: Come inside into the cool of the bar-room. One of the things that has sometimes seen me through a black square – this is a joke! – has been a stiff drink. Why do people invent such things? Why do people invent pleasures and rewards, but so that we can qualify immensities? It is not for us to start to ask the questions at the far end of wisdom, because we are not there. Even I am not there, and I certainly know more than I did when I was alive. One thing one learns is that a faith of some sort – in the tools, in the small things – is all.

Dilys: I think he's saying he did not have many possessions. Maybe he had things, but I don't think he was bothered about them. He's saying he didn't tie himself – and again, I've got Elgar. I don't know whether he liked Elgar, but I think he felt he and Elgar had some kind of connection – they were there together, sort of. I think he felt Elgar was very tied to his house – you know, his cottage -

Paul: Yes.

Bax: I never had that feeling for the ground. For me the world was endless and limitless. The places were visions in themselves – the bluebells – the cliffs – everywhere was a

103

vision in itself, wherever I wandered to I could see something in it. I could see the music in it, and it spoke to me, it said things. I never wanted to leave it, but I never felt it belonged to me in the way that I could put up a fence and say 'This is mine'. In many ways I was lucky, because I was not ripped – parted - from my physicality in that way. I found it perfectly natural to retreat into the spirit, because I had lived there so often in the music. I never had that sense of outrage that people might sometimes have if they are forced to give things up, so my comfort has come from the same comforts that were there all along - every time there are bluebells and blue flowers under those trees, every time the waves come in or the night falls, the comfort is there.

Dilys: I want to ask, are we doing the right thing, is this a new take on reality?

Bax: I leave that to you. It has not been easy to do this – perhaps not even a wise thing, but I have not claimed to be very wise. I want to do it. I want it to be said.

Dilys: I think that's it now, though I've still got the hotel, the place.

Bax: I really enjoyed living in a hotel – (**DG**: inn, whatever it was – a pub, he calls it). I really used to feel that I was everywhere and nowhere, I was everybody and nobody. For me this has got far more meaning, sitting in the bar with my drink – or upstairs in my room – this has far more security and meaning for me than going into some big mansion that I owned, wandering the rooms, feeling responsible for it. I feel safe here. I feel this was where my feet touched the ground.

Dilys: This was the place in Scotland, I think – or a hotel somewhere. It could have been several hotels together.

104

Bax: A pub, a hotel, a lodging, an inn, is for the traveller, and I was an eternal traveller. I'm still a traveller, so make of that what you like. Reluctantly, we say goodbye until the next time. Thank you for sharing these ways with me, because they are not ways that everyone would want to tread. Let who will share them and come with me – with us. They will have to find themselves. All I can do is be here and be ready, and this I do with my whole heart. So until the next time, we will be gone - To the Lighthouse. There! A literary allusion for those who like culture. (**DG**: *To the Lighthouse* is the title of a novel by Virginia Woolf, first published in 1927)

Dilys: He's very tired now. I'm going to say goodbye. And thank you.

10

BAX – THE HIDDEN MAN
Paul Gater

'There are parts of one's life - or one's existence – where no-one sees and you don't want them to see'
Bax

Bax was such a charming man, so easy to get along with, that those who knew him must have assumed it was very much a case of 'you saw what you got' so far as he was concerned. In fact, he was probably one of the most private people around, and the complexity of his music reflects this. Whatever assumptions have been made over the years since his death, his true worth as a man and a composer has almost certainly not yet been recognised. He talks here of his struggles to find and express the truths he wanted to convey – only to realise as he progressed that he knew less and less. Fresh examination of his work excitingly reveals these same themes reflected.

Emotionally scarred by the loss of childhood security, Bax in many ways never outgrew these traumas. One of the reasons his parents had removed to Ivy Bank, their large house with its glorious gardens in Hampstead in 1893, was the loss of Aubrey, Arnold's young brother, who had died of meningitis aged 10 while they were living in their previous home at Clapham Common. After the move, Arnold was to retain vivid images that lingered for the rest of his life, of the garden at Ivy Bank. He delighted in the fact that the family seemed to be living deep in the countryside instead of in a London suburb, due to the size and density of the trees and shrubs. Within the broad confines of terraces, spacious lawns and flower borders, he and his brother Clifford and sister Evelyn enjoyed playing as children and adolescents with their many friends and sometimes with members of the gardening staff.

Like ourselves, gardens evolve, go forward; but those of our childhood are transmuted into legend. For Bax, the garden at Ivy Bank where each season displayed magical delights to the growing children, offered all the freedom and security they needed within its boundaries. The 'cut off' point from this enchanted world came in 1911 when, on his marriage to Elsita, he moved from Ivy Bank to a house his father had purchased for the young couple in another part of London. Restless and unable to settle, Bax took his wife to Ireland; and sadly, it was that same year Ivy Bank was sold for demolition, subsidence having made serious inroads into the structure due to the construction of the Hampstead Underground Railway. Gone now and for ever was the garden that, to Bax, had been 'an island dream peopled with all the phantoms of adolescent dawn'.

Much that was vital to him was never conveyed to those around him, and perhaps could never have been communicated unless through his music or some other kind of imagery. For instance, though he apparently held no orthodox faith, it is obvious he possessed an intensely deep and almost mystical awareness which pervaded everything he did, but which he found frustratingly unable to share.

Imagery in fact proved greatly important throughout his life, whether musical, literary or visual. Paul Corder, a close friend and son of his composition teacher at the Royal Academy of Music, had invented a pioneering type of colour photograph and in 1907 took a picture of the 24-year-old composer. Considering that it was from a century back, it still looks as fresh as though taken a few days ago. (See end of this book)

108

Another image that Bax found endlessly meaningful and absorbing was of sunset, especially sunset over the sea. He was 6 years old in 1889 when, during a visit to Worthing, his parents took him to the top of Arundel Park – on this occasion he is on record as having witnessed what he described as his 'first golden sunset'. His life charts his progress from that 'first golden sunset' at Arundel through to viewing his last in Ireland on the very day of his death.

Another of the secrets Bax seems to have kept hidden so far as he could from others concerned his health. A heart-murmur having been diagnosed, he was regarded throughout his early years as 'a delicate child'; and in 1901, during a family holiday in Malvern, a doctor even told his parents he was suffering from acute heart disease with only weeks to live. The diagnosis proved quite inaccurate but caused them great distress, particularly as they had already lost one son: a second opinion was sought immediately. It set their minds to rest, but the heart murmur did persist throughout Bax's life. He was exempted from service in the First World War, and appears to have undergone incidents of chest pain, some reported by witnesses and others possibly suffered in private.

Characteristically, Bax refused to acknowledge his weakness. In his autobiography, for instance, he shrugs off the incident at Malvern, writing dismissively that on the day following the grim diagnosis he took part in a hard game of cricket in the grounds of Malvern College. It is obvious that he did not want to be considered any kind of an invalid: and we were very interested to note that early on in our communications, he behaved in exactly the same dismissive way. 'I was disgustingly healthy,' he insisted, when Dilys picked up that he had had chest problems.

From the early 1920s he gradually changed physically. From being slim (even painfully thin), he became rather plump and red-faced. This was probably due to his increasing intake of whisky – a habit which did not auger well for his health and could also have contributed to the falling away of his compositional gifts, particularly during the final decade of his life.

Bax obviously held a dual view of himself with regard to his awareness of fantasy and reality. While declaring that he did not agree with sentimentality or romantic notions - the 'Celtic Twilight', for example - he nevertheless continued to express himself in the most outrageously adolescent terms to the subjects of his affection throughout his life. Often the 'purple prose' in his letters can be embarrassing to read. Yet from the content of these 'conversations', it is clear that Bax's self-awareness was painfully acute and honest. Even though he might have tried to delude himself about his feelings particularly towards the young women with whom he became infatuated, he was always fully aware of what he was doing and knew the difference between what was real and what he wanted so desperately to believe was reality.

In many ways, it is this recognition of his own human frailties that gives Bax his stature as a person. From his first encounter at the age of 19 with the poetry of W B Yeats and the myths and folklore of Ireland, Bax remained faithful to them even though disillusion soon chillingly dispelled his far-off, secret and mysterious everlasting Celtic dream. On the one hand, this helped him to get through the changes and crises in his life. On the other, I think, they left him extremely vulnerable to 'the slings and arrows of outrageous fortune'.

When 1914 came, nothing could have prepared him (or the many others affected) for the traumas and terrible carnage of the First World War. Among personal friends who perished were gardeners from Ivy Bank, the poet Edward Thomas, the composer George Butterworth, as well as musicians he knew or had worked with who had played his compositions. Bax also felt deeply for those on 'the other side', having met many people during visits to Dresden in 1906/7. Compositions such as *In The Faery Hills, Into The*

Twilight and *Spring Fire* now seemed so far away from the grim reality.

Had it not been for his relationship with Harriet Cohen, Bax might have returned to Ireland in 1914 and on his own admission, would probably have become involved in the Irish Cause. In England he felt in spite of his personal happiness that he was 'living in exile'. But there were many friends he would never meet again in Dublin: in one way, Bax was now in the process of losing yet another garden, another place that had been so vital to his early adult life – Ireland, as he had known it. After 1918, he no longer felt an 'honorary Irishman' but merely a visitor whenever he returned to that country.

Some of the Irish Nationalists he knew, such as Padraig Pearse and the poet Thomas McDonagh, were shot by the British Authorities for their part in the 1916 Easter Rising in Dublin. News of the event came as a terrible shock to Bax, who was staying on the shores of Lake Windermere in Cumbria at the time. The same Authorities were to brand some of Bax's own poetry, in which he celebrated them as martyrs, as subversive, and this must have been one of those times that he truly was living on the edge of the world. For him it was a precarious situation and if it had not been for the grounding presence of his 'nymph' - Harriet - securely ensconced in his life, he might indeed have found himself, as he puts it 'tipped over the edge'.

It is interesting to speculate the outcome had Bax actually made that return trip to Ireland in 1914.

111

11
TO THE LIGHTHOUSE
In conversation with Bax – 5

Think, in this batter'd Caravanserai
Whose Doorways are alternate Night and Day,
How Sultan after Sultan with his Pomp
Abode his Hour or two and went his way.

Edward FitzGerald
The Rubaiyat of Omar Khayyam

Dilys: I'm just wondering where the lighthouse is. Which lighthouse it is. Or whether it's actually the lighthouse in Virginia Woolf's book, whether he knew anything about it. He's not here at the moment. (pause).

Bax: Yes, it is a puzzle, isn't it, as to where this lighthouse is.

Dilys: I've actually got a picture of it in my head. I don't know whether it's any real lighthouse – somewhere maybe off Scotland – or is Cumbria on the western side, the western coast, the west coast - ?

Bax: A lighthouse, yes.

Paul: I think it's a particular one in Ireland.

Dilys: Well, it seems on the left-hand side of the country – to the west – of wherever. I was thinking it was off England or Scotland, but it could well be off Ireland. The lighthouse is one that he saw, and knew.

Bax: I thought about it often later - afterwards. (**DG**: Does this mean, after his death?) I wondered whether the lighthouse really existed, or whether I had just imagined that it existed because I needed it. When I was looking out to the west – towards the Atlantic – I thought how terrifying it was, the prospect of infinity. I feel the same sometimes when I look at the music. I need the music – the scale, the notes of the scale – I need it in order to make sense. You have to hang on in this life to these small disciplines and restraints, otherwise you would go mad. Sometimes I wonder if I did go mad, perhaps. Not all the time, but when I looked at the prospect of that golden sea, I couldn't face it. The confusions that arise provoke nothing so much as sheer terror. That's why I like to play the piano, because the keys are under your hands and you have got control, you have the reins of life in your hands when you play the piano. I found there were many terrifying prospects in living -

Bax: - In what you call relationships. What did I call them – I don't know. I might have called them meetings – encounters. It's what they call relationships now. But what does that mean? In the same way as you look at the lighthouse, looking out into the infinity, I always felt I needed some kind of secure point before I could look at something like love. Love is like a sea, like a golden sea – you want to go there, but you are so terrified because you will lose your way – you have no idea at all how you are going to find your way, or even whether if you put your foot into the sea you will simply sink like a stone. Actually, I was never the confident person I seemed. I like to deal with things that are touchable.

114

Dilys: I have a picture of him – you told me, Paul, he used to play billiards – I have a picture of him holding a cue, touching the billiard balls.

Bax: I was very drawn to sensual things. I loved the world, I loved the things you could touch – the blossoms, the stones. It's when you come to these infinites that you can only be guided by something you can't touch, like a light. You can't touch a light. You can't touch the lit road, the hope. You can't touch these things. How can we deal with them? We are lost, we are utterly lost.

Dilys: I have a picture of him trying to see where he is. He seems to be standing on a cliff by the lighthouse, not far from the lighthouse. He's looking out to sea.

Bax: The lighthouse flashes all the time, I suppose, the beams (need) never stop. But when it's day time, and it's sunny, you just don't notice. It's a pulse – it's a pulse. The same thing with music. I suppose I must have tried to capture all this because this was what concerned me about life. I couldn't explain it or talk about it. I tried to pin it down by pinning down the things that one could control, like the pulse – how the light, the pulse, is like a heart-beat. It's something we need. If we didn't have that heart-beat that reminds us of our mortality, what would we have but complete and utter silence, complete chaotic silence? Music is very much something that structures the things we are unable to cope with without it, things that frighten us. Sometimes -

Dilys: (after a pause) A sort of block there. He's trying to think.

Bax: I was going to say, the music used to frighten me too, but no, I don't think music ever frightened me. You have to

115

look below music. To me music is very reassuring, for me it means the lines, the papers to write down my notes. It means the notes themselves, on the piano. I was never one of these composers who composed in some kind of dream world. I loved the feel of the keys, the touch – the pressure of my finger pressing down the key. Does anybody ever appreciate these days, the actual wonder of pressing down a piano key and producing a note? I used to find it amazing. When I first started to play – the first time I played the chords, I think I have told you – it was a miracle. To me, a miracle of three notes – the chord of C. Has anybody ever thought what a miracle a chord is? I never got over it, even though I went far beyond standing there and marvelling at what I could do when I played a chord. C Major.

Bax: - Music is something that is in your head, and in many ways it is untouchable, but I feel the mystiques (that's your modern word, mystiques) must be removed.

Dilys: There was other music - jazz music – Charleston – I have a sense generally of all the music that was around, that he might be referring to. I think he was quite interested in it.

Bax: Yes, I liked the dance music. I loved to listen to the beats - those beats – because they are the pulse. And drum beats of whatever kind, a regular beating.

Dilys: I have a picture of Ireland, with an Irish instrument playing, the Irish drum – I can't think of the name.

Bax: Everywhere I went I wanted to get back to that beat, because that was the thread for me, the beat of life, the heartbeat – the actual beat of something on something that produced the sound. I have no time for the theorists, the flannel-mouthed conversationalists who want to know things

116

about music which cannot be explained. I loved the beats - the dance music, I loved the Irish – the Gaelic music. I valued my hearing very much, and all the five senses to me were equally valuable because I lived through those senses very extremely. Music is actually your senses. Music is not something removed and in some dimension that only the elevated, the specially privileged can enter. Another thing – music is not money. A lot of people think – or thought – that music was for those with money. I want to put the record straight here. For me, money was a thing one could touch, it was something one needs the same way as you need the piano keys. It's like perhaps, like a drum. Money is the stick that touches the drum, money is the finger that presses down the key and produces the effect, to some extent. That is its usefulness to me, it's part of something which is necessary in order for the whole to function. I suppose I really was ruled very much by my perceptions through the senses, which I felt played through me as music. And money is one of them -

Bax: - I did like money, but its usefulness is what it could do. Music is not necessarily something that can be bought. Music is a great miracle of life, the great miracle of life. It's the sensuousness that I lived by and every time I touched the key, every time I wrote down a note, every time I composed a phrase -

Dilys: I can see he's actually talking now about the young woman, the pianist – Harriet Cohen. He's thinking about her, seeing her sitting at the piano. Very grave, I think she was rather grave.

Bax: Every time she touched the key and played what I had written, and she'd look up and smile, and – *that's music!!*

117

Dilys: He's very emotional now, very overcome by that thought. A Christmas card has come into my mind here - This picture of her sitting at the piano, and playing a note and looking at him and smiling.

Bax: What more precious gift could one have than to know that you have opened a gate, or a door, you've turned a key for someone so that you press a key and you write down a note, and they press the same key. It's beyond a sharing, it's beyond an anything.

Dilys: He's half-laughing now.

Bax: I think I was a softy, an old fool – maybe a young fool as well. I really saw life in colours, different colours to other people. The music was the brush through which I could paint the pictures. (pause) I would have liked to have painted her picture. I would have liked to have drawn or painted her (like this) somehow. But you can't hold it back, no more than when you press down the key, you must let it up again, because you can't keep (**DG**: He meant halt or bar) time, you can't stop time. It is so important, and time is so very relevant to music as well. In one way, there is no time in music, but in another, it has to be structured through time. This is what makes it bearable and liveable, this is what gives it its great immensity.

Dilys: I have a picture of steps, a long staircase.

Bax: What would a staircase be – we're back to stairs again, steps, and in a way the notes are like steps, the chords are steps – but what would a staircase be, a flight, if it never ended? It has to go somewhere. A staircase is a state of being which can only be temporary. You cannot live on the stairs always, and some people do wish they could. When I think of that moment (**DG**: Looking at Harriet at the piano) I wish I could stay on the stair for ever, that stair. But already the smile had faded and she had looked down again, and I could not hold it.

Dilys: This picture of her sitting at the piano, just playing something he had written, just playing the notes with her right hand and looking at him and smiling, is something that to him, I think, meant far more than any recollection of some great passion.

Bax: She could enter though the same gate, and she could tread - (**DG**: An image of footsteps in the snow) – I made the footprints in the snow but she could tread in them, and so it was that we could walk together. We went through a darkened forest. I could go through dark forests. I knew that she was there behind me, to catch me should I fall. (pause) A dark forest is a very frightening place.

Dilys: I have an image of thorn-bushes, black, thorny bushes.

Bax: I suppose these were my compositions, my compositions were going into the forest through the thorn-bushes, in the dark. - Christmas, and snow on the ground, I think. Lights behind in the house. But I would always be drawn to the dark night outside, the places where it was hard going. I could never be satisfied with the easy path. There is no path through a dark forest, dark thorns, covered with snow on them, blackthorns, the sort of fairy-tale forest that can represent so many things. I always wanted to go into the forest. Why, I don't know, don't ask me why. I did not want to go back to the house. It's easy to stay in that house with all the lights on -

Dilys: This might be him as a child. There's a house - that big kind of country house - with lights on in all the rooms, everybody celebrating Christmas. There was a lot of festivity going on, and he went out into the snow and walked, and made these footprints, and he saw – he's looking at them now.

Bax: You put your foot down in the snow, and you lift your foot and there is a patch that's dark. It amazed me how I put my foot down on the white snow and I lifted my foot – like pressing the note – and it left an image, it left a print, and the print was something else again, it had been transformed. It was packed ice, packed snow, and then it began to slowly darken, it began to fill with water. I could not believe what I could do by walking in the snow. I was making music by walking, pushing down my feet. I made music by walking on the snow, and I left notes – I left the notes on the snowy field - (**DG**: A long, wide kind of lawn with the trees thick beyond). The forests were where my music took me. But in the forest it was different, there was no snow and I couldn't see. I had no prints. It was very frightening, but – I was able to do it. Later I understood the necessity to walk on. And she was there and somehow, because she could tread in those footsteps, I knew she would pick me up, she would be there if I faltered and fell -

Bax: - Isn't that an amazing thing? Isn't it wonderful? Isn't life wonderful, isn't it all a miracle when you think about it? Putting your foot-print down in the snow – looking at a bird flying –

Dilys: I've got him suddenly reverted back to the coastline and he's watching the bird above the cliff. And now he's gone back to being older, he was I think mixing in with younger memories there.

120

Bax: Another way is, the white bird against the sky. A seagull is white, with black tips. That's the black and white notes. I see music everywhere. I saw music everywhere, and it flies and it moves, so perhaps this goes some way of explaining what life was like for me.

Paul: It's said that Elgar, when he went out in the country, could pick notes out of the atmosphere. He could hear them and put them down on paper. Was this very similar to the way Bax is describing?

Bax: No. Elgar and I were quite different. I did not hear them. I talk about the senses – my senses – I value very highly, my hearing I value, but for me, I did not hear a note until I had pressed down the keys. The notes I saw around me were my raw material, but there is only one note for me, that is the note when you press down the key. Otherwise, it's a bit like telling me that you walk in the country and you see the notes growing on trees. I find the idea rather ridiculous.

Dilys: He's laughing now.

Paul: No, I wasn't referring to notes growing on trees, I was referring to the possibility that Elgar picked them out of the atmosphere.

Bax: But how can you pick a note out of the atmosphere? To me it's a transmuting process. Perhaps I did so – perhaps I did so - To me, I was only able to compose when I was able to touch the keys. They finalised my thoughts. I did not hear music and then write it down, I brought it with me. I entered a state perhaps of trance, where I was aware of music all the time. I saw music everywhere. I saw music in things which are not sounds – in the birds flying, in the imprints – but it was only by sitting and concentrating on those keys that I was able

121

to put the music together. Perhaps in some ways, perhaps I heard it when I looked at the scene, but for me those drum-beats, those rhythms, those pulses, the keys, the pressures, are what makes the music. And let nobody tell you anything else, because there is no other way. It is not easy. You do not think of music in your head and somehow it becomes. You work to translate what you are given at that keyboard, in that room.

Dilys: I have him at his piano again, whichever room it was. I think he needed the piano to compose – obviously, he's saying so.

Bax: You live in a world of music, as one lives in a world of love, as the sea is limitless to the west. But how do you pick out one wave, or one feeling? To try to do so would be extremely arrogant. It would be unthinkable. Only by filtering through using the senses to translate it into something physical can one capture it.

Dilys: I'm asking him now about people singing – old songs – because he must have heard old folk tunes sung and played. I don't know whether he was interested in them – I don't think he really was – but he liked the procedures, I think.

Paul: I'm sure he heard a lot of Irish tunes.

Dilys: Yes, and I'm thinking of old Cornish tunes.

Bax: What was the difference – in Cornwall, for example – between hearing someone sing an old tune, or hearing the dripping of water in the tin mines? This is mystique again. Everyone works according to their gift and their own tools, and the process is a miracle. How can we take it on ourselves to be responsible? In many ways I feel I was a craftsman. I was not an inspirational, elevated conveyor of abstruse

122

philosophy through musical notes. I was a craftsman first and foremost -

Bax: Think about the Irish coast. Where is the music there? Yes, they sang, they played the instruments and they danced – they make noises with their feet – the Irish twist their senses. In their dancing they use the feet but not the hands. They will use certain elements and twist them round. That's why their dancing is so compelling, because it's structured and yet completely free. I tried to put that into the music too. There's a way of putting together the structure, the close confinement, very strict structures, and yet having the music flowing free as well. I saw this with a bird – the lighthouse - The lighthouse flashes, that's the beat. The bird is flying free above it, that's the free melody. How do we fit them together? I have no idea. It is a miraculous process, and for me the great joy of music was that it never ended. It was always there, it was always new, it was always fresh -

Bax: Do you hear the water dripping in the tin mines? And do you hear the sound of the hammers? People think I only put the sound of the sea into *Tintagel*, but they are there too. They are part of the Cornish coast. Who cares about an old ruined stone castle? It was not Tintagel I was capturing, it was the spirit of Cornwall.

Paul: To me, in *Tintagel* there was a very quiet, very haunting melody. I was wondering whether that referred not only to the Tristan and Isolde legend but to the tender feelings that ran between himself and Harriet.

(long pause)

Bax: I do not think I could have put that into music. It was always there in all the music. For Tristan and Isolde, there's a lot of mystique. To them perhaps, too, the sea that both brought them together and separated them was both free and yet structured. It had a rhythm and yet it was so infinite. I did not deal with abstruse emotion as such, I put down what I felt. I mean, in Cornwall, the lives of the miners and their loves — the little lanterns — were just as great as the great beams of the lighthouse, and those little twinkling lanterns and candles are just as miraculous as the huge sweep of the light. Tristan and Isolde — I never met them. I met her (Harriet). I knew her. I met them - the miners — the people, the ones who were there — very much in the moment. I do not write for mythology and long ago history. I look at it and I see similarities, but how can I answer for Tristan? I was not there. He didn't tell me how he felt. I saw what I saw. It's there all the time. Live in the moment, live in the now. Why bother to find what Tristan thought when there are a modern Tristan and Isolde walking up the path before you. Why try to discover what King Arthur did or said when you have a hero who is trying to save his people today. Perhaps I never expressed this at the time — it wasn't fashionable. But then, I was never very fashionable.

Paul: Perhaps he and Harriet were the then 'modern' Tristan and Isolde.

Bax: Young man, you are looking to the past. Do not do that. I am ancient history, and so is she.

Paul: Yes, but there was a time when he was 'modern'.

Bax: What is modern? When you are alive, you do not care whether you are modern or ancient. I have told you this. One does not think — am I historic, or am I *avante-garde*, or am I modern? You simply are, and you take the moment as it comes. Does a bird — the seagull — the black gull I saw — does

124

it think of what it is doing? The miracle of life is that you don't think about it – the miracle is that you simply are there, and you experience, and you feel with your senses. As soon as you start to think about what you thought a moment before, you have upset the whole procedure.

Bax: If I stopped and looked back to the bar that I had previously written, how could I write music? – if I stopped every time I wrote a bar and had a look at the previous bar? You flow on, you must flow, you must go where the tide takes you, you must follow it to the edges – wherever it takes you, however terrifying. But then again, life is all terrifying. Life is coming onto a sea – this golden sea – it is just as terrifying when one is born. It's a different sea, but how terrifying it must be, to think back to birth and to imagine what we felt like as we emerged into the world. Have you ever thought of that? Ponder on your birth, think about it – and think how unintelligible the world is to the newly-born spirit – how it needs lights, and it needs threads. (**DG**: He had previously used 'light' in regard to hope, and 'threads' as guiding disciplines)

Bax: I see life upside down, from another angle. If you wanted to do it, you could do the same. It is very easy for me to relate things to having passed to where I now am. You can't do that yet, but you can use your birth in order to give you a different view.

Dilys: I want to ask him about death, and see whether he has anything to say about it – what it was like to die.

Bax: I think for me, the far end of the - golden sun going down in the west – the far end for me was never reached. I was not aware of when I passed.

Dilys: I don't know how he died, but I think he must have died quite peacefully.

Bax: I was not aware of when I passed into the far west. (pause) Perhaps it would have been very interesting if I *had* been aware. Perhaps I could have written about that. But we don't need to know about it, it has its own music.

Dilys: Is there any particular message this time, like there was last time?

Bax: You've seen my emotion. It was for different reasons on this occasion, but equally it cuts one to the heart when you look at the person – as I looked at her. It's so painful. The experience is so deep and so painful that it is almost impossible to suffer it. My emotions were like knives. They cut me into pieces – or they would have if I had let them – and I feel reluctant to meddle with knives. Perhaps my message is to show you how un-trivial the trivialities of everyday can be.

Dilys: I'll ask him if this is enough for today. I'm seeing the big pink shell again, the shell that was on his desk. The golden sunset scene – the sun going down over the sea – is very much the image for this. He was by the lighthouse, but he's also on the cliff looking at the sunset sea – and it is golden, the sun flooding the quiet sea – not the breakers now, a quiet sea. He's showing me the pink shell again.

Bax: When you pick up a shell and listen, you can hear the murmur of the sea. That's why I kept a shell with me – near me -

D: Thank you.

126

EPILOGUE

*'One holds on to that thread and moves forward,
heading for the west and the twilight, the ending of the day'*
Bax

'TINTAGEL' BY BAX
(For Paul, with thanks)

*It was not from the coast
That I saw Tintagel
For the first time,
But from the 'Mermaid'
By the old beacon, in Staffordshire.*

*The Roaches served
Both as rock and castle,
And through the apportioned fields,
And calm little puffs of sheep
Sucked some force from
The imagined tempestuous scene,*

*Still the sky rolled
Like an upside down sea,
And fleets of cattle leaned
Against a southwest wind
That had kissed Cornwall
Only a few hours before.*

Mark Borg

129

We had approached our friend Mark initially with a view to including some of his photographs in this book: we felt they exactly captured the atmosphere and mood of Bax's word pictures. He read the first few chapters and was immediately hooked, the 'conversations' making such a deep and profound impression that this poem was the immediate result.

We feel each person who reads *Summer with Bax* is likely to react just as strongly. The experience of writing it has been for us a unique privilege, and Bax even kept the promise made in the title he had given us. The contacts commenced, as described in an earlier chapter, on the day before the Midsummer Solstice – the first day of summer – and though we were not aware of it until afterwards, the actual day we realised there would be no further communications from him and that the book was from his point of view finished, was the day before the Autumn Equinox - the last day of summer.

In the same way he crafted his symphonies, Bax presents here a new, mature work of amazing power and authority. It is skilfully constructed, bringing all his themes together finally, and rounded off – as his work often was - in a quiet conclusion.

We were not able to appreciate the intense significance of his closing words until much later. Paul discovered that he had spent his last days in Ireland judging annual music examinations. During what were to be his final hours, he had made a visit to the lighthouse on the Old Head of Kinsale, near Cork – a spot he had loved.

Throughout his life, Bax had felt his spiritual resources recharged and replenished through connections with nature – in particular with beautiful dawns and sunsets. During the course of his last day (3rd October, 1953), he spent some time looking out over the sea – his ocean, the Atlantic - and experiencing what would prove to be his final 'golden sunset'. A few hours later, with no premonition or pain, he was dead of a coronary thrombosis.

He parted company with us at the conclusion of this, our summer journey, in the same quiet way, leaving all who have travelled with us, and with him, a stirring challenge.

- 'Where are the companions who will come with me to the edge of the world?'

It is the measure of this man's greatness that he adds humbly: 'I hope there will be an audience there. I hope there is a listener. One always wanted a listener.'

Ah Love! Could thou and I with Fate conspire
To grasp this sorry Scheme of Things entire,
Would we not shatter it to bits – and then
Re-mould it nearer to the Heart's Desire...

And when Thyself with shining Foot shall pass
Among the Guests Star-scatter'd on the Grass,
And in thy joyous Errand reach the Spot
Where I made one – turn down an empty Glass!

Final stanzas
Edward FitzGerald
The Rubaiyat of Omar Khayyam

Paul Corder's photograph of Arnold Bax, taken in 1907
(By kind permission of Graham Parlett)

133

A SHORT MUSICAL
APPRECIATION OF
SIR ARNOLD BAX
Paul Gater

'The discoveries of the previous age have to be re-interpreted, re-explored.'
Bax

Despite an upsurge of interest in Bax's music, it appears that concert promoters (and some conductors) still assume the lesser known tone-poems and the longer works, such as the symphonies and the Violin and Cello Concertos, are no longer the 'crowd pullers' they once may have been. Their one 'fallback' seems to be *Tintagel*.

So on a recent visit to Chester, Dilys and I were delighted to see a poster announcing that Bax's *On the Sea-Shore* (an early piece from his abandoned opera *Deidre of the Sorrows*, orchestrated by Graham Parlett) was to be part of a forthcoming concert of works by British composers to be held in the Cathedral.

In the past, like most people, I only encountered a relatively small amount (mostly on records) of what this exciting, intriguing composer has to offer. The birthday centenary celebrations of 1983 triggered an invaluable number of professional performances of his works, probably enabling many people to hear a Bax composition for the first time in years, or even for the first time in their lives. But all this is changing. Now, thanks to record companies like Chandos, Decca, Epoch (Dutton), Naxos and others – new recordings and reissues (including historical) are happily becoming available. Reasonably priced, repeated hearings of a widening repertoire of his works are becoming a real option.

Asked for a 'way in' to appreciate Bax I would suggest considering the very beautiful *Quintet for Harp and Strings*, his early *String Quintet in G,* the three mature (numbered) string quartets, progressing perhaps to his other chamber works. The Impressionistic tone-poems, some of which have already been referred to, also have much to offer: *Nympholept, November Woods* and *Tintagel* being substantial enough in themselves to represent exciting, atmospheric symphonic movements. The very fine *corpus* of symphonies offers boldly unique experience, each in its own right a journey of the soul, once Bax's 'big' musical style is familiar to questing ears.

The four Piano Sonatas, written between 1910 and 1934, represent a lynchpin to all his compositions for the instrument (these are works I am currently exploring). His other pieces include an extrovert Two-Piano Sonata and a number of short, Impressionist works.

Though obviously this is not a comprehensive survey of Bax's music – more of an appetiser – we must briefly consider what I believe is the significance of another of his orchestral tone-poems – the intriguing *Spring Fire.* 'Swept up' by his interest in paganism, partly ignited by Diaghilev's *Ballets Russes* and verses by the Pre-Rhaphaelite poet Algernon Swinburne, Bax wrote this in 1913 as a freely worked 'symphony' in 5 movements, set in 'an enchanted wood'. Based on the first chorus of Swinburne's *Atalanta in Calydon,* it is a fresh recounting of a tale from Greek Mythology, the primitive and earthy connections and significance of trees inherent in the piece appealing very much to the composer.

Spring Fire was composed at the end of what used to be thought Bax's 'early maturity'. Because of the craftsmanship and imagination involved, however, I think this particular work forms an important link between a number of previous compositions (including the early tone-poems) and those that were to follow (for example, the 7 symphonies). The incidence of the First World War, of course, was to cast its own influence over everything that followed.

Spring Fire makes us realise that Bax had composed works of high magnitude far earlier in his career than has hitherto been assumed. Due to setbacks for various reasons over time, he was never to hear the work performed himself; and what might have meant this piece was lost for ever was the destruction of the original score in a disastrous fire at Chappell's, the music publishers, in 1964. Miraculously, reflecting perhaps its pagan roots in the cycle of death and rebirth, another copy (almost identical) was discovered in 1967 among Harriet Cohen's papers following her death.

Spring Fire was eventually premiered in 1970. Other performances followed, including a much-acclaimed recording by Vernon Handley and the Royal Philharmonic Orchestra. Handley's recordings of the symphonies with the BBC Philharmonic Orchestra in 2003 on the Chandos label, won a coveted 'Finalist' award from *The Gramophone* the following year.

In one of his 'conversations' Bax says that because we are too sophisticated these days, we have lost touch with the freshness and magic of existence. It could be said with regard to his own music – and to *Spring Fire* in particular, which has come down to us as 'new' (not the only, until recently, unperformed piece, but the most important) – that he is now giving us a completely fresh perspective on it all. He is revealing modern significance in what was once deemed 'old hat' – the 'shocking' poetry of Swinburne, lost legends, the pioneering work of Diaghilev, powerful imagery and particularly ourselves, all seem to stand glowing in an incredible new light.

As he says in another of his 'conversations': 'The sleeping often don't want to be wakened - because when they wake it's harder than being asleep.'

137

The choice is ours.

For me it is the excitement of listening to (and learning from) his music with this fresh insight. A poor performance of work by any composer can so readily promote indifference, Bax being no exception. Via *committed* performance, however, we cannot but help being swept along, going with him even to that very 'edge of the world'.

Inspirational yet eternally questing, youthful and yet wise, Bax has the potential to be many things to many people of all ages, and here is a composer for all time.

ACKNOWLEDGMENTS

It would have been impossible to research the background to this book without reference to the comprehensive works already in existence on Bax and his times. Thanks are due to:

Farewell, My Youth – Sir Arnold Bax (Longmans, Green & Co, 1943). A lively and illuminating introduction to the composer's earlier years.
Composers Gallery – Donald Brook (Rockliff, 1946)
Masters of the Keyboard – Donald Brook (Rockliff, 1947, 2nd Edition)

Much information by various authors and performers may be found on notes and booklets accompanying recordings of Bax's work on LP records, tapes and CDs, and we gleaned many facts and insights from these. Once again, thanks.

We would especially like to acknowledge our debt to *Bax – A Composer and his Times* by Lewis Foreman (Scolar Press, 1988 2nd Edition); and also to Richard R. Adams and Graham Parlett at the Sir Arnold Bax web-site:

www.musicweb-international.com/bax

The authors may be contacted at:
Anecdotes Publishing
Tel: 01538 373227
e-mail dawn@anecdotes567.freeserve.co.uk